Dear Reader:

The book you are about to read is the latest bestseller from St. Martin's True Crime Library, the imprint *The New York Times* calls "the leader in true crime!" Each month, we offer you a fascinating account of the latest, most sensational crime that has captured the national attention. *The Milwaukee Murders* delves into the twisted world of Jeffrey Dahmer, one of the most savage serial killers of our time; *Lethal Lolita* gives you the *real* scoop on the deadly love affair between Amy Fisher and Joey Buttafuoco; *Whoever Fights Monsters* takes you inside the special FBI team that tracks serial killers; *Garden of Graves* reveals how police uncovered the bloody human harvest of mass murderer Joel Rifkin; *Unanswered Cries* is the story of a detective who tracked a killer for a year, only to discover it was someone he knew and trusted; *Bad Blood* is the story of the notorious Menendez brothers and their sensational trials; *Sins of the Mother* details the sad account of Susan Smith and her two drowned children; *Fallen Hero* details the riveting tragedy of O. J. Simpson and the case that stunned a nation.

St. Martin's True Crime Library gives you the stories *behind* the headlines. Our authors take you right to the scene of the crime and into the minds of the most notorious murderers to show you what really makes them tick. St. Martin's True Crime Library paperbacks are better than the most terrifying thriller, because it's all true! The next time you want a crackling good read, make sure it's got the St. Martin's True Crime Library logo on the spine—you'll be up all night!

Charles E. Spicer, Jr.
Senior Editor, St. Martin's True Crime Library

SLEEP MY LITTLE DEAD HOW WE LOATHE THEM

When the subway jerked to a stop in East New York, it was 1:45 A.M., March 8, 1990. Mario Orozco limped out into the sub-freezing, early morning air, and began the ten-block walk to the modest home he owned with his sister. He did not notice a young man in dark clothing behind him, on the other side of Nichols Avenue, shadowing him on the otherwise empty block.

Just before Mario reached Atlantic Avenue, the man crossed the street on his blind side and came up behind him.

Bang!

Mario, a Scorpio, felt a hot sting in his back.

"You're killing me! Help!" he screamed. The sidewalk seemed to fly up and slam into Mario's side.

As he lay there, the gunman casually stepped over him, straddling him, and pointed the barrel of the gun straight at Mario's head. . . .

Robert Christiansen Jr.
TRUE CRIME

SLEEP MY LITTLE DEAD

The true story of the Zodiac Killer

Kieran Crowley

St. Martin's Paperbacks

SLEEP MY LITTLE DEAD

Copyright © 1997 by Kieran Crowley.

Cover photograph AP/Wide World Photos.

ISBN: 0-312-96339-4

Printed in the United States of America

St. Martin's Paperbacks edition/October 1997

10 9 8 7 6 5 4 3

For Riki and Ariel

ACKNOWLEDGMENTS

THIS is a work of nonfiction and is based on several thousand pages of police reports, confessions, court documents, press accounts—including an interview with the accused Zodiac Killer himself—and hundreds of interviews over a six-year period. Among those interviewed were victims and their families, witnesses, police, lawyers, prosecutors, and the mother and sister of the suspect. In addition to my own reporting on the case for the *New York Post*, I reinterviewed many of the principals in the case, as well as dozens of others. Experts in psychiatry, handwriting, ballistics, and astronomy were also consulted.

While researching this book, I located a forgotten Zodiac Killer witness, whose testimony may become significant at trial, and discovered evidence that I believe is the missing link between the biblical, astrological, and satanic aspects of the infamous serial murders. All of the above led me to form a theory that I believe may solve the one remaining mystery about the Zodiac Killer—how he knew the astrological signs of his first four victims.

There are no fictional or composite "characters" in this book, although some real people, including several witnesses and Zodiac Killer suspects, were given pseudonyms—which are denoted by asterisks the first time the name appears. Several key steps and details were omitted from descriptions of weapons construction, to ensure that it is not possible to make a gun from reading this book.

Certain events, sequences, and conversations were necessarily reconstructed from a synthesis of all the evidence, including the alleged confessions, police reports, interviews with participants, and other information. It is important to note that the accused Zodiac Killer is innocent until a jury finds otherwise. His lawyers have challenged the validity of his alleged confessions and that issue is still pending in court.

First, I would like to thank my editor at St. Martin's Press, Charlie Spicer, for all his help. I would also like to thank my literary agent, Jane Dystel, who had confidence in me, even before the events of June 18, 1996, gave the Zodiac Killer drama a third act.

The *New York Post* is almost a personality in this book and I am grateful for all the help from my many colleagues. I would like to thank Editor Ken Chandler and Metropolitan Editor Stu Marques, who allowed me to take leave, on short notice, to write this book. I am grateful to Head Librarian Laura Harris and her staff, who were indispensible. Thanks to Associate Photo Editor Gretchen Viehmann, who located many photos for this book. Also, I want to express my gratitude to several reporters who told me what was left in their notebooks after they wrote their stories, including: Susie Forrest, Bob Hardt Jr., Angela Mosconi, Allen Salkin, and Eric Sturgis.

I am very grateful to Eddie Seda's mother, Carmen Gladys Alvarado, who invited me into her tidy apartment for an extensive, emotional interview, during which she discussed her son and his home life from childhood onward. She showed me her son's room and allowed me to look through his belongings, books, and papers. I want to thank her daughter, Gladys ''Chachi'' Reyes, as well, for all her assistance and her honesty. I would also like to gratefully acknowledge the help of Eddie Seda's defense lawyers, David Bart and Alexandra Tseitlin, who have been gracious and considerate.

The office of the Brooklyn District Attorney has my thanks for their assistance and I acknowledge the assistance of the office of Queens District Attorney Richard A. Brown, in gaining access to public documents and records. I am obliged to NYPD Police Commissioner Howard Safir and Deputy Commissioner of Public Information Marilyn Mode, for their help, as well.

This book could not have been written without the co-operation of many police officers and detectives involved in the case—especially Detective Sergeant Joey Herbert and Detectives Louie Savarese and Tommy Maher—who ended the Zodiac Killer saga by putting the cuffs on a suspect. I am indebted to them.

Retired Deputy Chief John Menkin, retired detective Lieutenant Mike Ciravolo, and retired detectives Ray Liebold and Bill Clark, as well as Al Sheppard and Jim Tedaldi, were there for the start of the Zodiac Killer investigation in 1990, and I thank them all for their help. Also, I am thankful to all those sources who gave me their confidential help—whom I am unable to thank publicly, for various reasons. My thanks also go to the surviving victims, especially Mario Orozco and Jim Weber.

Forensic psychiatrist Dr. Michael Welner, MD, gave me an education in the workings of a serial killer's mind, as well as other invaluable suggestions, for which I am grateful. My thanks also to a friend, child abuse investigator Eddie Arredondo, MA, MSW, for his help and insights. I thank handwriting expert Charles Hamilton, who rendered an opinion on the Zodiac Killer's handwriting. Gregory Matloff, Ph.D., professor of astronomy at New York University and the New School for Social Research, was my navigator through the constellations of the Zodiac Killer case and he has my stellar thanks for all his help.

Words cannot express my gratitude to Al, Tess, and Kathy Nemser, for all their help, proofreading and support. Lastly, none of this would have been possible without the love and patience of my wife, Riki—my toughest editor—who kept me pointed at the right star.

—April 18, 1997.

Chapter 1

FAUST IN BROOKLYN

EDDIE was seated at the small wooden desk in his room, a table lamp lighting its surface. He had lived in the room, with the same furniture, since grammar school and the ten-by-twelve-foot room still looked like the home of a very neat sixth-grader. Nothing was out of place. His legs, clad in black pants, barely fit under the tiny desk, which faced the white wall. To his right was a long, low chest of red drawers that still had his Boy Scout stickers stuck onto the front.

Eddie was twenty-two years old and only left his room for a few hours each night. He had no job, no wife or girlfriend. He had no friends. He had only his work.

Open before him was one of his most prized possessions, a large piece of heavy paper with white dots and lines on a huge black circle—a star chart of the constellations in the heavens.

Framed by black, arched brows, his brown eyes were focused on the star map, eyeing the white spots and faint lines that connected them into the ghostly, floating figures of the zodiac. Eddie's black T-shirt and pants made his untanned olive skin seem lighter than it was. His curly black hair was pulled tight behind his head into a small ponytail and gathered with multicolored rubber bands. A full black mustache and rough half-growth of beard covered half of the smooth skin of his boyish, handsome face, which bore an intense, angry expression.

One more time, he spun the dark circle of sky, until he was looking at the stars and constellations for that night after midnight, May 31, 1990. Orion the Hunter and the Pleiades—the Seven Sisters—were safely below the horizon but Leo the Lion was loose in the sky.

Good. Perfect.

On the desktop, over the star chart, Eddie carefully spread out his school supplies—a blue ballpoint pen, a green felt-tipped pen, white paper, a compass, and a ruler—as if he were beginning his geometry homework. Nearby, wrapped in a piece of paper, sat three large pebbles.

He pulled on a pair of black leather gloves. From a plastic package, he removed a sheet of white looseleaf paper with five punched holes down the left margin. School paper. Using the compass and pens, he carefully drew and wrote his message on the page.

When he was finished, he folded the paper several times around the stones and drew something on the outside. Then he wrapped the package in another sheet of paper. He took off his gloves and put most of his writing supplies away into their drawer, arranging the pens and compass in an orderly row. He left out one green felt-tipped pen.

Eddie's drawers were very neat. All of his clothes and books and papers and toys were stacked and aligned properly, the same way every time, with the corners of some things pointing to specific letters or spots on the object below. Only his bureau was locked, but it didn't matter. If anyone ever went through the books or magazines in his closets or his files, he would know because they could never replace them exactly. The booby-trapped stack was a trick he had learned while studying to be a secret operative.

His dream of being a U.S. Army Special Forces commando never came true because he was an only son. They would not take him into the army and give him a real gun of his own—because he had failed their tests and because his mother did not want to be left alone. But just because Eddie had to stay with his mother in East New York, Brooklyn, one of the most crime-plagued and drug-infested neighborhoods in the city, didn't mean he couldn't be a commando. It certainly didn't mean he would cease his quest for knowledge, especially if it was forbidden or hidden.

He turned and glanced at the red numbers of his clock radio, 12:02 A.M. It was time. He stood, turned around, and walked a few steps to a wrought-iron and wood table that held a twelve-inch color television. On a low shelf below the televison sat a cedar box emblazoned with a cross inside a circle. Eddie opened the casketlike box and removed the white leather family Bible. Numerous mass cards from funerals Eddie had attended, as well as slips of paper, were used as bookmarks and protruded past the gilt-edged pages.

On the wall above the TV hung a church calendar, with a bow of dried palm fronds received in church on Palm Sunday tucked into the top. To the right of the calendar was another set of four shelves, which contained more religious materials. A second Bible in Spanish belonged to Eddie's mother, but he used it often. Several religious medals were also displayed, including a commemorative Pope Paul bronze medallion.

In a place of honor, on top of the Spanish Bible, was a red five-by-seven-inch paperback book, *The 6th and 7th Books of Moses, or Moses' Magical Spirit Art.* The cover featured an engraving of Michelangelo's marble sculpture of the prophet Moses. In this version, the two horns on Moses' head were very prominent and devil-like and the Hebrew holy man stared back with sorcerer's eyes.

The book was filled with several works on white magic and black magic and offered the sorcerer's apprentice page after page of magic charms, cabalistic circles, and secret incantations to call up spirits eager to do his bidding. A treatise from 1850 on astrological influences and magical cures stated that the ancients believed that "the heavenly bodies were gifted with life and that they, being endowed with higher powers, could exercise an influence upon man by means of mysterious magical influences, could regulate his temperament, his disposition and his term of life." One part of the book was devoted to necromancy, the art of speaking to the dead in order to predict the future and grant wishes. There were complete instructions, some by the legendary magician Faust himself, on how to conjure up demons like Mephistopheles—the devil. Another section was devoted to the magical use of the Psalms of the Bible, which, combined with certain arcane rituals, would secure all manner of help for the user, it said. Small scraps of paper had been used to mark certain pages, and important rituals had been circled or marked. The white pages were stained in several places with oils and what appeared to be blood.

Eddie took his Moses book off the shelf and placed it, along with the white Bible, on the desk. He sat down and opened the Moses book to page 161, where he had left a clean piece of paper as a bookmark. The name "Faust" had been scribbled in the margin of the book next to a passage on the magical use of one of the Psalms:

You should write the 83rd Psalm properly, upon pure parchment, and suspend it around your neck, and by so doing you will abide safely in war, avoiding defeat and captivity. If you should, however, be overcome, your captors will not harm you, for even in captivity no harm can befall you.

Eddie opened the white Bible to the 83rd Psalm, picked up a green felt-tipped pen, and carefully began to copy the words of the Psalm onto the loose piece of paper. He smiled to himself as he copied the line about the enemies of the Lord that "have taken crafty counsel against thy Hidden Ones." Like Eddie. The words of the Psalm implored God to make the enemies perish and become "as dung for the earth." When Eddie had finished, he poked two holes in the top of the paper and threaded a black shoelace through it and hung the talisman around his neck.

He stood and walked past the television to the corner of his room, to his cabinet of curiosities, a dark walnut bureau with two large doors. He unlocked it with a key from his pants pocket and pulled open the left door. Inside, hanging from a bar near the top, were Eddie's night clothes, including a black jacket, his maroon Omega beret, and other dark apparel, all in proper size order. Below the hanging clothes were several pairs of black shoes and sneakers and a pair of dark leather boots, with 2½-inch heels. He slipped on the jacket, then sat on the end of his bed and pulled on his boots, zipping up the sides above the ankle. Eddie's small bed was barely big enough for his wiry frame. Neatly made, it was covered with a pink satin quilt and two pillows decorated with large matching pink roses.

Taller now, he stood up and put on a black navy watch cap, like a SEAL commando before a mission. He tucked his black leather gloves and a spare hat into his jacket pocket, along with a small black penlight, and then pulled open the right door of the bureau, revealing an open shelf area above four drawers. A dozen shiny cylinders sat on the open shelf—stacks of silver quarters.

He pulled open the second drawer and pored over his glittering collection of knives, all arranged side by side, like in a store or museum. Also decorating the drawer were his razor-sharp ninja throwing stars, his brass knuckles, and military insignia.

He selected a sheathed dagger and pulled the gleaming 3½-inch blade from its scabbard to make sure it was spotless before he slipped it inside his belt. He closed the drawer and pulled open the one below it.

Unlike the sparkling weapons above, the drawer contained rows of dull gray metal pipes that were strung with loose brown shoestrings and heavy rubber bands and wrapped at the ends with white adhesive tape. Some had wooden handles. The objects looked like pieces of scrap metal or make-believe plumbing thrown together by a child. In the back of the drawer was a row of small, square cardboard boxes, each of which contained 50 bullets of .22-caliber, .38-caliber, 9-millimeter, or .380 automatic rounds, all with soft-nosed lead tips. Eddie took two spare 9-millimeter bullets, squat brass cartridges topped by fat lead slugs, and slipped them into his pants pocket, in case he was followed. He fondly regarded his clunky creations and selected one heavy, foot-long pipe that had a T-juncture and a protruding six-inch piece of pipe in the middle, the shorter piece of pipe wrapped in white adhesive tape. He picked the object up by the short, white handle. A commercial logo, "U.S. Pipe" was molded in raised letters on the middle fitting. Eddie liked that because the large letters "U.S." reminded him of the U.S. Army.

Eddie glanced up at the wall to the right of the bureau, where four wooden shelves displayed plastic models he had constructed years ago. On top was a large aircraft carrier, a battleship below that. Two models of jet aircraft were nose-to-nose on the third shelf, and the bottom shelf held a tank and missile carriers. They were empty toy missiles, war planes that would never fly, warships that would never sail, or even float. As a child, growing up without his father, Eddie enjoyed assembling the hundreds of tiny pieces. He liked working alone in his room, slowly, painstakingly, and still did. The best part was when he would show his mother a completed model. She would beam with pride and make a big fuss over him, calling him by his nickname, Herri. She praised his talent and skill and even bragged to visitors about her smart son. But, after her next husband arrived, and, later, Eddie's half-sister was born, his mother had less and less time for him. Even when that husband left, like the others, it was never the same.

The make-believe guns on the models would never fire, but the one he made with his own hands from junk did. What would his mother say if she knew?

He placed the weird weapon into the left inside pocket of his jacket. He then took the twice-wrapped message from his desk and put it into another pocket.

He picked up the Moses book to refresh his memory. Everything must be done exactly right. He turned to the marker for page 152 and scanned down the page to where "Faust" had been written in the left margin and a drop of oil stained the page next to one familiar entry:

PSALM 20—Mix in a vessel, rose-oil, water and salt, pray over it seven times in the most holy name Jeho, this Psalm and a suitable prayer, in a low voice and with reverence, then annoint with this oil your face and hands, and sprinkle it on your clothing, and you will remain free from all danger and suffering that day. Are you summoned to appear before the judge in person, in a judicial trial, you should avail yourself of the above means shortly beforehand, and by so doing you will surely be justified and depart without restraint.

Eddie did an about-face and walked to the outside wall of his room, to an oval mirror with an ornate dark wooden frame hanging on the wall. It had once hung lower on the wall, so little Eddie could dress for school, but it had been raised so a 5-foot-8-inch Eddie could now see himself in the glass. Below the mirror was a child-size wooden table with a small bowl partly filled with water. Next to it were a salt shaker and a bottle of rose oil. Into the bowl he poured some rose oil and sprinkled some salt, and mixed it with his finger.

Every move he made was reflected in the glass, as if two Eddies were at work. The letters on the sign around his neck were backwards in the mirror and seemed mysterious, like the magic of the ancient Hebrews in the book.

He picked up the white Bible and opened it to a bookmark. He began to read Psalm 20 of David in a low and reverent voice, low enough not to wake his mother and sister, who were asleep in the next room. Seven times he intoned the words of the Psalm, an ancient battle hymn whose music had been lost long ago. The words called on God to protect His anointed and implored Him to "accept all thy offerings, and accept thy burnt sacrifice."

Eddie felt a deep, rumbling wave approaching, coming up through his feet, building, coming closer. He let it flow through his entire body. The room began to shake and rattle like a gentle earthquake from the subsonic vibration of the subway four stories below the floor, beneath Pitkin Avenue. Slowly, the earthquake subsided as the train passed.

He felt a cool draft on his face. A soft May breeze of spring air was wafting through the two large windows on either side of the mirror. Both windows opened onto a metal fire escape outside. The wind was billowing the curtains decorated with big, fat blue roses that matched the sky-blue sections on the patterned cobalt-blue linoleum floor. The flooring was old and worn through in several spots, but had been mopped at least once that day and sparkled with cleanliness.

Eddie stepped to the barred windows, which were covered with an ugly lattice of steel security gates, to keep out criminals. But the breeze didn't smell like roses of any color; it stank like East New York. Through the metal, he looked out of the crumbling century-old building he lived in, at an almost identical building next door. Looking up, he could barely see a little patch of midnight sky, but no stars. Too much pollution, too many lights. But the stars were there—even in the daytime—guiding our destiny, even if nobody could see them or bothered to look.

Eddie felt another wave building inside him, but this time it wasn't the subway. It was the feeling, as if the spirit of Zodiac was entering his body. He could feel hot, red rage emanating from his groin, building, flowing upward, tightening his stomach, anger and pain and fear enflaming his heart and face, in shivering wave after wave. Soon, he would find a new victim to fire it into. He would spread fear. He let the anger flow through him and pass. He was in control. He could control it because he kept himself pure. He was not a sinful fornicator. He had never had sex with anyone. God knew that.

Wearing his high-heeled leather boots, he was as tall as the San Francisco Zodiac, which made it harder to identify him by height. Since there were no prints on the letter in his pocket, the cops would have to believe the California Zodiac had come to New York.

Very soon the anger would flow through him again and it would be harder to control. Only one thing could satisfy that feeling, and the time was right, according to the stars.

The only ones who could stop Zodiac from bringing forth the twelve signs—one victim for each astrological sign—were Orion and the Seven Sisters, and they were not in the sky. But Eddie's sign, Leo the Lion, was prowling the sky above, protecting him, giving him power. Just like the other times.

It was time for Zodiac to strike again. Zodiac would follow his next target. He would punish the sinners and his message would be known.

Eddie anointed himself—his unshaven face, his black hair and black clothing—with the holy liquid and strode out into the night of the new day, smelling like a rose.

Chapter 2

THIS IS THE ZODIAC

JOE walked slowly, painfully slowly, his chronic arthritis allowing him to take only small, shuffling steps along the filthy sidewalk of Jamaica Avenue. Joe wore his life on his face. His pain and bitterness had twisted the once-handsome features downward into a permanent cranky frown. His pace was punctuated by the slow, steady movement of his cane across the concrete of East New York, Brooklyn. His dark eyes under bushy brows were fixed on his path, his prominent nose and jutting chin angled downward, intent on the task. Joe was dressed more for winter than for a cool, clear, fifty-degree spring night the day before June. He was bundled in a gray sweater and scarf and plaid coat, a blue hat covering his full head of silver hair. He left his home in nearby Queens after midnight, as usual, to walk and rummage through the trash cans on Jamaica Avenue for a readable newspaper. Why buy one, when you can get it for free? But more importantly, Joe was looking for food among the trash. He received only about five hundred dollars a month from Social Security and his rent alone was three hundred dollars. Joe went out at night because he still retained shreds of pride and didn't want people to see him picking through garbage and taking food. With all the delis and diners on Jamaica Avenue, some of the stuff wasn't so bad, like the partially eaten sandwich he had just pulled out of a can and stuck in his coat pocket. He'd look at it later in the light. If it wasn't too old, he would eat it. It might be better than cat food. Next to the rotting sandwich in Joe's pocket was a small piece of cardboard, on which Joe had neatly printed his name and address, one of many such handwritten "cards" he would hand out. Losing a battle with senility, Joe would often forget his own address, as well as other things, like his name. But he remembered his boyhood clearly and his mind often wandered through the happier past, especially alone late at night, rather than spending time in the painful present. In his other coat pocket, Joe carried his keys and a small brown plastic notebook that he used as an address book and memo pad. The entries were pathetic testimony to Joe's illnesses, loneliness, and the temporary nature of his memory. His name and address, as well as the names and addresses of doctors and estranged relatives, each appeared over and over on the pages, the few names filling most of the book. The pages documented his arthritis, painful hernia, varicose veins, constipation, and his longing for happiness and release from pain. He paraphrased comforting biblical psalms that counseled him to "not trouble, neither be ye terrified . . . the Lord your God is he that goeth with you to fight for you against your enemies, to save you." and "Lord is they sheperd [sic], they shalt not want. Bring us to green grass and clear water . . ." In the secrecy of his own diary, Joe, not a poetry kind of guy, penned a rambling verse in a cramped, arthritic hand. It was trite, didn't make much sense, and the spelling was bad. But it was Joe's personal prayer—and would prove to be his epitaph:

> Live for what we are, not what others think we
>   should do.
> Do without our hearts and go by blood in your
>   veins.

Some sunny day, when the stars are shineing
  [sic] bright
That will be the day that everything will be
  alright
On that sunny day.
When that day will be, no one will know, you
  or me,
On that sunny, sunny day.

Joe tried to save on food because it enabled him to buy
a few cans of cheap beer, which helped to ease the burning
pain in his joints, which wasn't so bad on a nice night like
tonight. But nothing would restore the agility and strength
the retired seventy-eight-year-old once used to clean these
very sidewalks as a city street sweeper or heft huge chunks
of ice as a deliveryman. Joe's hands, also afflicted with
arthritis, made difficult his one hobby, drawing.

Eleven days earlier, Joseph Proce had celebrated his sev-
enty-eighth birthday, which meant his astrological sign
was Taurus the Bull. Joe was as stubborn as a bull and
paid no attention to astrology or his neighbors' warnings
about his habit of walking the streets at all hours. He had
made it through World War II without a scratch, and dismissed their concern with a wave of his rough hand. All
he really liked now, besides beer, was taking his walks,
day and night, doing errands or just walking. Some neighbors didn't tell Joe they thought he liked his beer a bit too
much, and behind his back they said senility, not Bud-
weiser, was the real reason he acted nasty and talked
strangely. Joe had a brother in Florida and an ailing sister
and other family in Queens, but he rarely spoke to them.
He never married and lived alone. The same neighbors also
wondered whether being alone so long, emerging late at
night to wander the streets, was healthy. They wondered
whether he should be in a home.

Joe slowly shuffled east on Jamaica Avenue under the
steel subway el that seemed to stretch away endlessly into

the dark. As he ambled, a distant rumble got louder until it became the familiar roar of a J train thundering over-head. Brilliant sparks, arcing from the third rail above, flashed through the metalwork like lightning, illuminating the darkened stone crypts and graves of the Victorian-era Cypress Hills Cemetery a few feet away, behind a black wrought-iron fence. If Joe had turned to look back during the pounding reverberation of the passing train, he would have caught a glimpse of a slim, muscular man dressed entirely in black, who had emerged from the shadows of the cemetery and was now following him. As the electrical strobe lit up overgrown mausoleums and mossy marble statuary in the dark graveyard, it also lit the pale, gaunt face with dark, staring eyes that seemed to float, disem-bodied, before the pitch-black boneyard.

Zodiac.

The train passed and the spotty streetlights were again the only light along the almost-deserted avenue. Joe ram-bled across the traffic-free street to the southern side and Zodiac followed.

Joe slowly moved past a shuttered florist and a mortuary stone mason, who made their livings catering to the dead of the sprawling necropolis nearby, which consisted of Cy-press Hills and a dozen other adjacent cemeteries on the border of Brooklyn and Queens. Some of those laid to rest there may have died victims of the horrific murder rate in East New York, among the highest in the city that year. But only a few living in the poor and working-class neigh-borhood could afford to be buried there. In fact, the only rich or famous people in East New York were dead. The 142-year-old Cypress Hills was the final resting place of celebrities like baseball great Jackie Robinson and magi-cian Harry Houdini, entombed in the one box from which he could never escape. Cypress Hills even had Hollywood stars underground, such as Edward G. Robinson and Mae West. West was interred in a white satin-lined casket inside an Art Deco mausoleum—clad for eternity in her trademark platinum wig and a jeweled white negligee.

Occasionally, the breeze wafted the living scent of flowers, mown grass, and trees from the cemeteries across Jamaica Avenue, which reeked of cars and subways and other stale, lifeless odors. The unlit cemeteries were some of the few places in East New York where, when the obscuring city air permitted, it was possible to see stars. On clear, moonless nights, you could see constellations like Joe's unheeded Taurus the Bull, or Leo the Lion, which hunted silently overhead, although they could not be seen from Jamaica Avenue. Orion the Hunter and the Seven Sisters were safely below the horizon. Just like the other times. Zodiac often hid in the graveyard that sloped above the avenue, to look up at the stars and down on potential victims.

It was hard for Zodiac to follow his target, only because Joe moved so slowly past the dark storefronts covered by padlocked metal gates, stopping to browse at almost every garbage can. Suddenly, near Mount Hope Cemetery, with its huge black iron gates emblazoned with the Star of David, author of the Psalms, Joe turned around. He retraced his steps back toward Brooklyn before heading east again, toward Queens. It was not the first time Joe had been shadowed by Zodiac, who also enjoyed drawing, the Psalms of David, and prowling the streets late at night. Until she died, Joe had also lived with his mother. He had no wife, no friends, and was lonely and in pain, things Zodiac did not know—or care about. Joe was simply a target. This morning, or, rather, yesterday morning, the horoscope for Leo, for Zodiac, in the pages of the *New York Post* was encouraging:

> Don't let others' negative attitudes, petty minds or lack of vision get you down. Mars in Aries after tomorrow highlights travel plans and all forms of communication. Therefore, if ever there was a right

time to paint on the broadest possible canvas in life,
then this surely must be it.

After six or eight blocks, Joe entered Woodhaven,
Queens, and turned right onto 75th Street. Joe moved so
slowly, the quick-moving Zodiac had plenty of time to
circle around the block and approach his prey head-on. Joe
noticed Zodiac for the first time as he moved south on
75th Street. Zodiac was walking north toward him. They
were alone on the otherwise deserted street. As Joe turned
right again into his block, 87th Road, Zodiac silently followed him into the neat, one-block street lined with trees
and once-grand old two-story town houses.

It was 2:00 A.M., May 31, 1990.

Joe picked up his pace slightly, once he realized he was
being followed, but his younger stalker had no trouble
quickly eliminating the distance between them. The elderly
man arrived at the ornate black wrought-iron gate in front
of 74–27 87th Road, where he lived in a cluttered, roach-
infested basement apartment. Zodiac was right behind him.
Excitedly, checking again to make sure they were alone
on the quiet block, Zodiac felt in his left jacket pocket for
his wrapped letter. Zodiac unzipped his jacket and reached
across his stomach with his right hand and grasped the
handle of the weapon in his belt. He was ready. As Joe
opened the metal gate and stepped inside the small paved
front yard, Zodiac stopped a few feet away and politely
spoke to him in a calm, gentle voice:

" 'Scuse me, can I have a glass of water?"

Joe was startled and turned to face Zodiac, who looked
at him with piercing eyes. The bottom of Zodiac's pale
face was dark with a mustache and a growth of beard.
Zodiac's unblinking eyes locked onto Joe's and stayed
there. Joe may have muttered something about getting the
glass of water, as he turned back toward the stairs down
to his apartment and safety.

"Can I come inside?" Zodiac asked, stepping into the yard with Joe.

"Why do you want to come inside?" Joe asked nervously, noticing Zodiac's right hand was inside his jacket.

"I'm cold," Zodiac replied.

"Where do you live?" asked Joe.

Zodiac answered that he lived not far away.

"Well, why don't you go home and get water?" said Joe with finality, turning again toward his stairs.

"Gimme a dollar," Joe heard Zodiac demand.

"I have no money with me. I have money in the apartment," Joe responded, panic in his eyes and his voice. His back was toward Zodiac, his cane pulling him closer to home, now just a few feet away.

At the mention of money, Zodiac's eyes flashed with fury and the anger began to flow. Perhaps the elderly man misheard Zodiac, who might have been saying he would give Joe a dollar for a glass of water, rather than demanding money, as Joe believed.

Joe turned his back on Zodiac for the last time and Zodiac's gloved hand pulled his lovingly handcrafted creation from his jacket. The thing didn't look much like a gun. It looked more like a piece of bad plumbing than a murder weapon. Zodiac held the homemade handgun in his right hand, his arm extended and pointed straight at Proce's back. With his gloved left hand, he pulled something at the back of the weapon and let it go.

Crack! The noise of the shot slapped off the stone walls of the small block, waking a dozen neighbors, most of whom ignored it and went back to sleep. Joe collapsed onto the pavement.

Zodiac did not panic. He had two more pieces of business to complete. First, he withdrew the carefully wrapped package from his left jacket pocket and placed it on the steps, ignoring his motionless victim. That done, he checked the glowing digital watch on his left wrist. It was 2:04 A.M. He would write it down later. He then thrust his hands back in his jacket pockets and walked at a quick but normal pace west, toward Eldert Avenue.

Down the block, while Zodiac and Joe were talking, two people had emerged from a house and into the empty street. The woman was now standing in the street, giving a good-night kiss to her boyfriend, who was sitting in his car. She turned to look toward the sound of the shot. Zodiac spotted her and darted between two cars to the south side of the street, and around a tree. She got a brief glimpse of the gunman as he hurried past, the only person other than Proce to see Zodiac's face.

On the second floor of a building on Eldert, the single shot alerted a neighbor, Herbie Block*, who recognized it as a gunshot and looked out his front window. Block saw a man, all in black, on the sidewalk below, "walking away with his hands in his pockets, like nothing happened." He watched the man stride casually toward Eldert Avenue, which runs north and south, perpendicular to 87th Road. If Zodiac had looked to his right as he reached Eldert, he would have seen the elevated subway line on Jamaica Avenue two blocks north, and the dark cupola of Franklin K. Lane High School behind it, but Zodiac turned south on Eldert. As soon as he rounded the corner, Block saw the man run "very fast all the way down Eldert" and vanish from sight. Several neighbors were already dialing 911.

"Help me."

Joe was not dead. The .38-caliber slug tore through his lower back, perforating a kidney and his lower bowel before exiting his abdomen. Dark, shiny blood soaked the front of Joe's stomach and groin.

"Help me," Joe whimpered again, dragging himself on his stomach across the concrete toward the main front steps of the town house leading to the first-floor apartment of his neighbor, Alice Lang*. Joe pushed himself erect with his cane, staggered up the steps, and rang Alice's doorbell. When Alice opened her door, she saw Joe talking to Block, who had thrown on his clothes and run down the block.

"Help me. I've been shot," Joe said, as his neighbors gaped fearfully at the blood on his clothes and smeared across the cement at his feet.

"I don't know why he shot me. I never hurt anybody," Joe said weakly, trembling now with shock and dizzy from loss of blood.

Joe was already changing his story. First, he said it was a Puerto Rican guy who shot him and then he said it was a black guy. Initially, he said there was no reason for the assault and then he said the man tried to rob him. He was the kind of witness that gave detectives ulcers.

"That motherfucker," Joe muttered, as he was lifted into an ambulance. He was scared and did not understand he was critically injured and would need emergency surgery at Jamaica Hospital.

"Just give me some aspirin, I want to go home," he pleaded with the paramedics, who had arrived with their siren blaring, and bandaged Joe in the flashing red light. Joe feared the ambulance would take him from his home and he would never return. Was he afraid the ambulance was his ride to his green grass and clear water, to his "sunny, sunny day" when the stars would shine brightly in the sun?

Did he also smell roses in the air?

After Joe was placed in the ambulance, Alice Lang gathered up his cane and the unclean clothes removed by the paramedics, and placed them in a neat pile inside his entryway. The back of Joe's coat had a bullet hole in it big enough to poke your finger through. On the steps, she noticed a paper note, like the ones Joe was always writing to himself. But this one was strangely heavy, weighted down with three small stones inside. When she opened it, she saw the single sheet of paper, which contained two large circles and some writing:

This is the Zodiac the twelve sign
Will die when the belts in the heaven
are seen

In the pale light of the street lamp, Alice's brow furrowed in confusion, as she squinted at the strange circles and symbols and the weird writing. At the bottom of the page was a large, crudely drawn circle-divided-by-a-cross symbol. Was it a Celtic cross, like a stone grave marker in one of the cemeteries?

Within a few weeks, that obscure symbol at the bottom of that letter left on a front stoop in Queens would seem more like the crosshairs of a gunsight, aimed at the heart of the city.

Chapter 3

NO MORE GAMES

EDDIE rubbed the scrub brush quickly and vigorously back and forth over his leather boot, the plastic bristles making an annoying grating sound. He was working over the white bathroom sink, in front of the mirror. On his left was an old white tub hidden by a red plastic shower curtain. In the other corner of the immaculate bathroom was a white toilet beneath a shelf bearing equally spaced bottles of shampoos and cleaning products.

After a mission, Eddie always ran straight home and jotted the date, location, and exact time in a small green spiral notebook in his bureau. Then he would go right to sleep.

At seven the next morning, he would wake up and make his pink bed smartly—like an army bunk, except for the pink satin quilt and crisp pillows with pink roses. Then he would say his morning prayers and begin scrubbing and cleansing his boots. After that, he would wash his black clothes and spruce up his already spotless room.

Like a good soldier, he removed any trace of mud or dirt, or anything else that might have splattered on his footwear. Using a cleanser, he kept scrubbing and scouring and buffing long after any spots remained visible on the leather or on the heel or sole. He really couldn't help himself. He began the same sequence on the other boot and worked until it shone.

When done, he washed and dried his hands, picked up both boots, and walked through the kitchen. Brilliant sunshine poured in through the windows on the right, near the dark wood-grain kitchen table. Thriving green ivy and red coleus plants lined the windowsill, but the view through the open windows was of the blackened bricks of a burned-out hulk, an abandoned section of the city-owned building he lived in. Three stories below was the barren dirt and broken pavement of the building's entry courtyard, where plants and shrubs no longer grew. The spotless white linoleum floor, white stove, white sink, white counters, and white refrigerator glowed in the spring sunshine. The top of the refrigerator was covered with several sets of carved, nested wooden eggs—painted doll figures that fit inside each other. Glass and brass étagère shelves next to the refrigerator held a stereo and a menagerie of many more brightly colored figurines, as well as a collection of dozens of ornate china pieces that overflowed onto the adjacent counter. All were arranged by rank and file, in symmetrical displays, like in a store or a museum. Even a collection of refrigerator magnets was spaced in an orderly pattern on the front of the appliance.

He continued into the tidy living room, which looked like a boutique with furniture. It was darker than the kitchen, since it had only one window on the right, near the kitchen. A long brown couch, behind an oval glass table, and two large red chairs were covered with plastic slipcovers in a style once jokingly described as Pitkin Avenue Renaissance.

A corner table, end tables, even the top of the couch were covered with silk flower arrangements and dozens of stuffed animals and dolls in elaborate costumes. The walls were covered with a few framed pictures and deflated, brightly colored birthday balloons.

On the right, as Eddie returned to his room, were white

french doors that led to what once was a dining room but had long ago been converted into a second bedroom, where Eddie's mother and half-sister slept. The glass of the doors was covered with white paint. Above the doors hung a large, old sabre. The windows of that bedroom were at a right angle to the living room and faced out into the courtyard toward Pitkin Avenue. Visible from the living room, above the carved walnut headboard of his mother's bed, was a crucifix above a landscape painting of the countryside with green grass and clear water, a scene far from East New York.

Eddie replaced the shining boots in their proper spot in the bottom of his bureau. In a drawer nearby was a thick, brown psychology textbook, which Eddie had studied. He had circled several paragraphs, in an effort to understand himself. One paragraph on page 505 said obsessive-compulsive solutions to the problem of anxiety "most frequently occur in intelligent persons with relatively high social status." This response to anxiety was "intellectual, less direct and primitive than a neurosis such as hysteria," it said.

Eddie cleaned and lubricated his weapon with 3-In-One oil before replacing it in the bureau. Then he cleaned and mopped his room before returning to the bathroom to shave and shower.

Three days.

It was Friday, June 1, 1990. Eddie decided to give the cops three days to put it together and announce to the press that Zodiac was at large in East New York. If he did not see something by Monday, he would take action.

On Monday, Eddie was angry. It had been five days since the shooting of the old man with the cane and not a word in the papers or on the TV news. How many guys do you have to kill before it makes the papers? Three targets aren't enough? He went out to buy a *New York Post*. A quick flip through the pages told Eddie it contained nothing about his nocturnal activities. He hurried home over broken sidewalks, past abandoned buildings that had become crackhouses, their walls laced with graffiti. Drug dealers had even begun to infest his own dirty brick building, and their apartment was one of the few oases of cleanliness and godliness left in the neighborhood. But on some nights, the evil of East New York would creep under the red door like a biblical plague. Pungent clouds of crack smoke, issuing from an apartment next door, would invade the sweet-smelling kitchen.

When he got home, he went into his room and shuffled through the pages of the paper again. Nothing. Why? The anger began to flow. Confused, furious, he stopped at page 58, "Your Horoscope" by Patric Walker, for Monday, June 4, 1990:

LEO (July 24–Aug. 23): The period immediately prior to the full moon in Sagittarius on Friday may be challenging, emotionally upsetting and prove that you have been led up the garden path. But, regardless of emotional dramas or outbursts, the whole shooting match has to be faced head-on.

Exactly. The pigs were playing games. The anger was flowing but he must control it. How could he face it head-on? He could go around them. If the cops wouldn't tell people, Zodiac could. If the cops wouldn't release Zodiac's letters to the press, Zodiac could. He could spell it out for them. Just like in San Francisco. But first, he washed his hands, to remove the disgusting gray newspaper ink.

Eddie ordered a lot of books and magazines by mail that reflected his special fascinations with guns, bullets, gun making, bombs, bomb making, sex, war, nuclear war, UFOs, devil worship—but especially murder. Some of his favorite book titles, other than the Bible, were *Hunting Humans* and *Serial Slaughter*, both large books that detailed the crimes and perversions of hundreds of serial killers. Another book almost certainly part of his collection was a book called *Zodiac*, about the serial killer in California in the late 1960's, who was never caught. The original Zodiac stalked and shot people at night and wrote letters to the San Francisco newspapers, bragging about his murders and taunting police. He said the people he killed would become his slaves in the afterlife. On the cover was the Zodiac's trademark symbol, a cross over a circle.

The book even had lists in the back that were meant to identify possible suspects but were very useful for a serial killer in search of an identity. The lists, which included the types of supplies, notepaper, guns, bullets, and knives used, were a brief course in how to become a Zodiac Killer.

Eddie took out his school supplies and arranged them neatly on one side of the desk. Out of the bureau he took three small slips of paper with dates and times scribbled on them. He arranged them carefully by date on one side of the desk, like fortunes from fortune cookies. He put on his black leather gloves and sat down. Sitting at his undersized desk always made Eddie feel big, almost like a giant.

He took out a clean white sheet of paper and began another message, writing, drawing, and using his compass. He copied the information from the slips of paper onto the page. He underlined the names "Zodiac" and "Faust" three times, each line smaller than the one above it, as if the names were at the top of a tornado.

When he had completed the message, Eddie examined the letter and was pleased with the results. With his gloves still on, he took out one of the prestamped envelopes he had purchased the previous year at the local post office and never touched directly. The postage in the top right-hand corner was a navy blue square with the letters "USA" in the center, but that was not why Eddie chose it—it was for the ring of thirteen stars circling "USA." One for each sign and one for Zodiac.

He then addressed the envelope "to The Editor, New York Post," with the 210 South Street, Manhattan, address of the newspaper. Eddie did not include his return address. The envelope looked bare as a result, so Eddie added the Zodiac's return address in the lower left-hand corner—the cross-and-circle Zodiac symbol. That's how the original Zodiac did it. After he had folded the letter and inserted it into the envelope, he licked the flap, sealed it, and stuck it inside the folded *New York Post*. Now it could be dropped into a mailbox without him touching it, without anyone seeing him mail it.

He took off his gloves, put away his writing supplies, and took the original paper slips into the bathroom. He dropped the crumpled paper evidence into the bowl and then he flushed the toilet. Like a cruel giant, towering above, he watched the three strips swirl around and go down the drain, like a trio of spinning white ghosts in a whirlwind. They have reaped the whirlwind because they were sinners. In the Bible, in Revelations, there was a warning to repent, or else "I will come on thee as a thief, and thou shalt not know what hour I will come upon thee." Amen.

To ensure success for his venture, Eddie returned to his room and opened his Moses magic book to page 166, to one of the circled entries:

PSALMS 110 and 111—The first of these Psalms is marked with the holy name Jah, and by its frequent use in the form of a prayer, a man may compel all enemies and opposers to bow to him and beg for quarter and peace.

He opened the white Bible to Psalm 110 and, over the starry envelope, gravely began to intone the words of David, in which God promised to "make thine enemies thy footstool." As he chanted, some of his words were loud enough to be heard throughout the two-bedroom apartment, but his mother and eleven-year-old sister, who had long before stopped listening, were not home. "The Lord hath sworn and will not repent, thou art a priest for ever after the order of Melchizedek," Eddie continued. "He shall judge among the heathen, he shall fill the places with the dead bodies . . ."

Eddie's earnest voice carried beyond the fluttering blue roses of his curtains, out the open windows of his room— where it was swallowed up by the sound of a television game show from the apartment next door and voices and laughter from the street below.

When he had completed the secret spell, Eddie picked up the newspaper with the letter inside, tucked it under his arm, and walked out into the afternoon to send his message.

Chapter 4

NOW WE HAVE A PROBLEM

DETECTIVE Sergeant Mike Ciravolo parked his car outside the 112th Precinct on Austin Street in the Forest Hills section of Queens at 7:00 A.M. on the morning of May 31. As he walked toward the station house—known to cops as the One-Twelve—in the early morning sunshine, he inhaled the fresh spring air and glanced up at a bright, blue sky. It was going to be a beautiful day.

The forty-year-old Ciravolo had seen a lot of action on the job before he changed out of a uniform and into a suit. In 1972, as an active young Street Crime cop in upper Manhattan, he got into a gun battle with a bad guy and shot him to death. Two years later, he stopped a bullet with his right thigh during a shoot-out with a youth gang. Close to retirement after twenty-two years on the force, he was still a handsome and trim guy with brown eyes and a distinctive cleft chin, but his hair was thinning on top and his black hair and mustache were turning gray.

Ciravolo strode up the stairs to the second-floor Detective Squad room and poured himself a hot cup of coffee from the eternally boiling coffeepot. Nightwatch Detective Anthony Cardamone, who had been up all night, was waiting for Ciravolo with a shooting from the midnight tour.

Joe Proce was shot about a hundred feet inside the borough of Queens and was the responsibility of Queens detectives. If Proce had hit the pavement a hundred feet west on Eldert Avenue, the case would have been the headache of the overworked Brooklyn detectives in neighboring East New York. Uniformed cops had responded to the 2:00 A.M. shooting, along with nightwatch detectives, including Cardamone, whose job it was to turn the case over to detectives on the day tour, some six hours later.

Because it was a presumed robbery and doctors at Jamaica Hospital expected Proce to survive, the case was not one for homicide detectives, but a routine robbery investigation for the Senior Citizens Robbery Unit, known by its initials, SCRU, and pronounced "screw." That meant it was the headache of Ciravolo, commander of the SCRU unit, who assigned it to Detective Ray Liebold, who had just walked in the door.

Ray Liebold, forty-seven, close to retirement himself and the father of five children, was not known as a high-profile detective, but as an unsung, hard-working investigator who often had to negotiate with the city Department of Social Services and other agencies to get help for his elderly victims. Sometimes, he felt more like a social worker himself when he had to reach into his own pocket to put food in the empty refrigerator of a battered and traumatized senior citizen robbery victim. It was gratifying when an investigation was successful and he locked up a predator who had viciously beaten and robbed helpless old folks, but there was no glory, no press coverage.

After handing off the case to Ciravolo, along with a typed DD-5 report on the shooting, the victim, and the witnesses, Cardamone added a verbal postscript before going home.

"There was one strange thing," Cardamone told Ciravolo, handing him a piece of paper inside a plastic sheet. "There was this note. There were a couple of stones holding it down on the front stoop."

Ciravolo looked at the note with Liebold, who felt a chill, like a cold hand on his spine, when he read it.

"This is really bizarre," said Ciravolo, as he handed the page to Detective Bill Clark, one of several other dayside detectives pressed into service for an examination of the shooting scene and a canvass of the neighborhood.

Clark, forty-six, who had served on the detective task force that caught "Son of Sam" serial killer David Berkowitz in 1977, had acquired a reputation among fellow detectives as a sharp, thorough detective with a talent for eliciting confessions from "perps," short for perpetrators. The affable, clean-shaven Clark, with his neatly trimmed light brown hair, oval face, and dimpled chin, had a friendly Irish cop's face that concealed steely blue eyes, which took everything in.

"Oh, shit!" exclaimed Clark as soon as he saw the message.

It was written on a sheet of white looseleaf paper with five holes punched in the left margin. There was a large, perfect circle drawn at the top of the page. A ruler had been used to draw three lines from the center of the circle to its circumference, making three slices out of the circle. Inside each, a different symbol had been drawn and they had been numbered outside. The first was a serpentine letter *M*, with a pointed tail at the end. The second symbol was the Roman numeral *II*, and the third was a circle with horns.

> This is the Zodiac the twelve sign
> Will die when the belts in the heaven
> are seen

Slithering to the right, the letters *S* were large and distinctive, like snakes poised to strike the other letters. Below the strange words, the name "Faust" was written in green ink and underlined twice. At the bottom of the page was a smaller, cruder circle with a cross inked over it, creating a third odd symbol.

Clark felt an eerie sense of déjà vu. It reminded him of

the Son of Sam case and the spooky letters the killer sent to police more than ten years earlier. This Zodiac, he thought, was like Son of Sam "when he threw down the gauntlet. A guy has challenged you and he's told you he's going to do more."

Ciravolo was outwardly cautious, but he also thought the note was extraordinary and he wanted to get to the crime scene as quickly as possible.

En route to the scene, Clark warned Ciravolo that if the note was from the gunman, he might have a serial killer on his hands.

"Mike," said Clark, "if this is the perp's note, make sure you do everything you can."

Ciravolo, already thinking along similar lines, agreed with Clark, whose meaning was obvious—it might be another Son of Sam and the biggest case of his career. Pulling out the stops was the right thing to do. Besides, if it was a serial killer, God help the detective, or detective sergeant, who failed to do everything he could while the case was fresh.

When they arrived at the scene, Ciravolo began directing the detectives, who were knocking on doors and speaking to neighbors. Discarded plastic surgical gloves and wrappers from bandages and other items left by paramedics who had aided Proce littered the sidewalk. An Emergency Services truck arrived and uniformed officers began combing the block for evidence, looking in yards and peering into sewer gratings for a discarded weapon, without success.

The Proce apartment was filthy and full of roaches. Rancid odors assaulted Liebold's nose when he entered the dank, sunless residence.

After finding Proce's cane and placing it inside the apartment, Clark examined the victim's soiled pile of clothing. He picked up the coat perforated by a bullet hole and shook it gently. A small lump of lead fell out onto the pavement. That was good news. He picked it up and examined the spent slug, which seemed to be a 9-millimeter or a .38-caliber round. Cradling the bullet in his open palm, Clark noticed it was not very deformed after passing through the old man's body. It was also oddly smooth, without the usual markings left on a bullet after its explosive passage out of the rifled barrel of a gun. That could mean it was fired from a homemade zip gun or antique smooth-bore weapon.

While Clark placed the bullet in an evidence bag, Liebold pulled a moldy half-eaten sandwich out of the old man's coat pocket, along with several notes and a small notebook with addresses and some strange writing in it. Ciravolo then sent Liebold to the hospital to interview the victim.

The canvass produced neighbors who were mostly earwitnesses who heard the shot, not eyewitnesses who saw the shooting. That left police with Herbie Block and the woman and her boyfriend down the block.

Block saw the shooter, but it was dark and the suspect was about thirty yards away. His look was not good enough for a lineup. Bad news.

The woman witness down the block and her boyfriend were the only ones other than Proce to get a good look at the gunman's face, which was good news. The bad news was that the boyfriend was married to another woman. Consequently, he did not want to go to court and explain in public what he was doing there that night. Both reluctant witnesses would prove to be of little value.

Liebold was unable to interview Proce, who had undergone emergency surgery and was in critical condition at Jamaica Hospital. Until they found out otherwise, it was still possible that the old guy wrote the odd note himself.

By 11:00 A.M., Ciravolo was back at the One-Twelve, which also housed the office of the commander of all Queens detectives, Deputy Chief John Menkin. Ciravolo walked down the hall to see Menkin, fifty-seven, who had a reputation as a low-key, tough but decent boss with a gift for understatement.

"Chief, we may have a problem," said Ciravolo, as he handed Menkin a copy of the note and gave him a brief rundown on the case.

"I hope we don't have another Son of Sam," said Ciravolo, when he was finished.

"All right, Mike," said Menkin after examining the letter. "Keep me posted on everything on this case. Keep me informed."

Also back at the office, Clark, on an NYPD voucher sent to the Documents Section lab, described the troubling message as a "satanic letter." Was the weird circle-and-cross symbol on the folded paper supposed to be a grave marker, a gunsight, or some other, darker occult symbol?

The detectives did not yet know that the crudely drawn circle-divided-by-a-cross symbol was a notorious emblem of violent human sacrifice on the West Coast. It had not been found by cops at a shooting scene in almost two decades, not since the Zodiac serial killer vanished from the San Francisco night.

A few days later, Liebold began a series of maddening interviews with a shaken Joe Proce in his hospital bed in the intensive care unit at Jamaica Hospital. Joe was not just a bad witness, he was worse than no witness at all. At least he was certain about two things: He did not know the gunman and he did not write the "satanic letter" left on his stoop.

"That's not me. I don't know what it is," Proce said, when shown the Zodiac note.

After Proce gave differing descriptions of his attacker, as both black and white, Liebold decided to try an experiment and pointed to a black nurse in a white uniform.

"Joe, what color is that nurse over there?" Joe turned, squinted at the woman and turned back to the detective.

"She's white," Proce said.

Liebold was upset but not completely discouraged. He

knew the shock of the attack had not worn off. He hoped Joe's mind would clear and his memory would return. But what if his eyes were bad? Without a reliable victim or witness, Liebold would have to make the case himself from the ground up. He was used to it.

But Liebold's hopes faded when he returned to the hospital the next day, and Proce looked at him with a bewildered expression and asked him the same question he would ask every time he saw him:

"Who are you?"

Terrific, thought Liebold, feeling a pang in his stomach. But it was only indigestion. The ulcer he got from the Job had been cured years ago.

On June 6, a strange letter, postmarked in Brooklyn two days before, arrived at the headquarters of the *New York Post* at 210 South Street, on the East River in Manhattan. Like thousands of other letters, it was addressed to "The Editor." It was opened by a copyboy. Since the letter bore odd symbols and purported to be about murder, it was forwarded to police reporter Anne Murray at "the Shack," the *Post*'s small office inside police headquarters.

The letter was written in blue ink on a white piece of paper, which was dominated by two circles. At the top right of the page, a neat circle had three pizza slices carved out of it, each with a different astrological sign. On the top left was the crudely drawn circle and cross that looked to Murray like a telescopic sight on a hunting rifle. Below the circles, the strange, unpunctuated words began:

This is the Zodiac the twelve sign
Will die when the belts in the heaven
are seen

The first sign is dead on March 8 1990 1:45 AM
White man with cane shoot on the back in the street

The second sign is dead on March 29 1990 2:57
   AM
White man with black coat shoot in the side in front
   of house

The third sign is dead on May 31 1990 2:04 AM
White old man with cane shoot
in front of house

To the right of the list was penned the name "Faust,"
which was underlined three times, just like the name "Zodiac" above. Beneath that was scribbled "No more games
pigs," which was underlined dramatically with an incom-
plete Z, like Zorro on a bad day. At the bottom of the
page, the author added further proof:

   all shoot in Brooklyn with .380 RNL or 9mm
   no grooves on bullet

Murray set about the task of finding out if the mysterious letter was just another missive from a twisted mind or
was actually correspondence from a killer, a tabloid reporter's fantasy-come-true. If it was true, she wanted to
keep it exclusive. Headquarters at One Police Plaza was a
notorious sieve. She tried to keep it close to her vest and
away from the other reporters in adjoining second-floor
offices by calling detectives she knew. The initial results
were disappointing. Murray was told there were no such
murders in Brooklyn. It looked like her big story was too
good to be true, but she faxed a copy of the letter to a few
detectives, who promised to check it out.

From experience, especially on the Son of Sam case,
Bill Clark knew how the combination of grinding hard
work and dumb luck could make or break a case.

Two weeks after the Proce shooting, Clark, working on
another case, walked into the 109th Precinct Detective
Squad room on the second floor of the station house on

Union Avenue in Flushing, Queens. As he passed a detective's desk, he caught a glimpse of something familiar—the cross-and-circle symbol from the Proce note. He thought it was a copy of the Zodiac note.

"What's this?" Clark asked, reaching for the note, which he saw had the same pie chart and symbols but a lot more writing, a whole page full.

"Nothing," replied the detective, turning the confidential note facedown. Clark laughed and turned the page over again.

To Clark's amazement, the detective explained that he and several other detectives were separately investigating the different Zodiac note, which had been sent to the *New York Post*. The note was bogus, he said. There were no such homicides in Brooklyn.

"These shootings don't exist," the detective told Clark, leaning back in his chair.

"Bullshit, I handled that," responded Clark, pointing to "The Third Sign" shooting near the bottom of the letter.

In fact, they were both right.

Reading through the new message, Clark experienced the heady feeling that detectives call "the Rush," an elating sense of discovery and excitement.

The date for the third sign was May 31, at 2:04 A.M., the date and time of the Proce shooting. As the note said, Proce was white, used a cane, and had been shot in front of his house.

He was puzzled by the claim that all victims were shot "in Brooklyn," until he remembered Proce was plugged just a few yards outside of Brooklyn. Maybe the shooter was a Brooklyn boy who didn't know he had crossed into Queens.

Clark was convinced he was on the right track when he saw the last line, "no grooves on bullet." He remembered the smooth slug he shook out of Proce's coat.

But the letter said all three were dead, and Proce was alive. Maybe there are two bodies out there, but maybe he's wrong about that, too, thought Clark. Maybe the shooter didn't stick around to make sure his victims were dead.

This is the real deal, Clark thought to himself. His heart pounding, adrenaline pumping, he picked up the detective's phone and called Chief Menkin. The last time Clark had called a chief was when mobster Carmine Galante got rubbed out while dining al fresco at a Brooklyn restaurant.

"It looks like we have a serial killer," Clark told Menkin. Clark then called Ciravolo.

"I just hope you did everything on the Proce shooting," Clark began. Ciravolo had, and he had a stack of "fives" and lab reports to prove it. Clark faxed a copy of the new Zodiac letter, along with Anne Murray's phone number, to Ciravolo's office.

At Detective Borough Queens, Ciravolo was on the phone, waiting for the fax, when he looked up from his desk to see Chief Menkin standing over him. A stone-faced Menkin dropped the faxed copy of the letter on the desk.

"Mike, now we have a problem."

Ciravolo called Anne Murray and made her day. He told her the letter might be genuine. An excited Murray agreed to hold the story until detectives could locate the other possible cases.

After they failed to locate any murders that fit the bill, Ciravolo directed Liebold to check first-degree assaults with a firearm. Liebold, working with detectives in the 75th Precinct, located two nonfatal, previously unconnected shootings on March 8 and March 29 in the same area that appeared to be the ones claimed by Zodiac.

Chief Menkin and Lieutenant Dan Kelly, brainstorming with an astrological wall chart, made the disturbing discovery that Zodiac knew the astrological birth signs of all three victims. Menkin said "a light bulb went on" in his head when he compared the birth dates of the victims to the astrology chart and the Zodiac note.

"Hey, Dan, look at this. Look at the signs of these people," said Menkin.

"What?"

"Look at the letter and the chart. The zodiac signs are in order, going around the wheel."

"You're right, Chief," said Kelly, confirming that the first victim was, indeed, a Scorpio, which matched the squiggly *M* with a pointed devil's-tail symbol in the pie chart on the Zodiac letter. The second, a Roman numeral *II*, was a Gemini, and the third, Joe Proce's Taurus the Bull, was symbolized by a circle with horns.

"Dan, what's your sign?" asked Menkin, his eyes sparkling with mock malice, making a joke that would soon be repeated all over the city.

Kelly just smiled, shrugged his shoulders, and refused to divulge his sign.

Joking aside, Menkin was very concerned. He knew he had a serial shooter who was preselecting his victims. But how did Zodiac know the birth signs of his victims in advance?

Anne Murray got her story. Half of the front page of the *Post* for Tuesday, June 19, was a picture of the eerie Zodiac letter. "Bizarre Letter Links 3 City Gun Attacks . . . RIDDLE OF THE ZODIAC SHOOTER" was in large, black type on the other half. The story, on page 7, revealed that the previous victims were two Hispanic men who had been shot in the back and the side. Television, radio, and the other papers picked up the yarn, and it quickly became the hottest story of the summer.

That same morning, Chief of Detectives Joseph Borrelli called Menkin, Ciravolo, Liebold, and several detectives from the 75th Precinct to an urgent 8:30 A.M. meeting in his corner office on the thirteenth floor of headquarters in Manhattan. The purpose of the meeting, in the rarefied atmosphere of One Police Plaza, was to find out who had what on the Zodiac shooter. Also to be determined was who would get the case, since two detective commands were involved. Careers were at stake and Borrelli was not happy. So far, the best information on the shootings had come from the press.

Borrelli, a former Queens detective, had experience with high-profile serial killers who liked to embarrass the police in the press. As a detective captain, Borrelli was also on the Son of Sam Task Force and was mentioned in one of the vain, taunting letters Berkowitz left at the scene of a shooting. Borrelli was pleased that the killer left his fingerprints on that letter, which became part of the overwhelming evidence against Berkowitz.

Before the meeting, three Major Case Squad detectives consulted on the occult case had told Borrelli that Zodiac was a copycat of the original California killer, and was shooting at twenty-one-day intervals. There were twenty-one days between the first and second shootings and the Proce shooting came exactly three cycles, or sixty-three days after the second one. They predicted that Zodiac would shoot again the next night—after Wednesday turned into Thursday, June 21, at midnight. Zodiac liked Thursdays.

Unfortunately for the detectives from Brooklyn, it quickly became clear that they had been elected sacrificial lambs.

Borrelli asked a detective lieutenant from the 75th Precinct Detective Squad what his investigators had developed in two months on the two shootings in their area.

"It's not much," he was forced to tell Borrelli, opening two thin folders with a few DD-5 reports, which chronicled the bare facts of the shootings and the difficulty in reaching the reluctant victims to reinterview them. Since both men survived and could not identify their attacker, the latest DD-5s had recommended the cases be closed. When the lieutenant finished, Borrelli was not smiling. He then asked Ciravolo what his detectives had unearthed in the last three weeks.

Ciravolo opened a fat folder, bulging with "fives" and lab reports, including fingerprint checks, a ballistics report on the Proce slug, and a Documents Section report on the note. The Queens detectives, who were already developing suspects, had also come up with the twenty-one-day theory. Zodiac might be poised to strike the next night, which meant there might be an opportunity to set a trap.

Borrelli scolded the Brooklyn lieutenant, saying those under his command were not thorough. Several at the meeting thought it was unfair criticism, but no one voiced the opinion.

The "Seven-Five" Precinct had something like four hundred shootings a year and about a hundred homicides, not to mention the volume of rape, robbery, and burglary cases. The two shootings had nothing to connect them, the victims could not identify the gunman, and no notes had been found.

"Mike, I'm giving you the case," Borrelli told Ciravolo. The Chief of Detectives dubbed the effort to grab Zodiac "Operation Watchdog" and promised Ciravolo additional detectives and other support teams. Ciravolo asked that the reinforcements report to the 102nd Precinct in Queens at 11:00 P.M. the following night, to set the snare.

"We'll bag him tomorrow night," Ciravolo predicted confidently.

Later that day, a cop at the Seven-Five Precinct in Brooklyn saw the Zodiac letter on the front page of the *Post*. It looked very similar to a wacko letter that arrived in the mail at the station house the previous November. That letter had also included an astrological chart and threats of murder by someone calling himself Zodiac.

The talk in the precinct that day was that the copy of the Zodiac letter that had been saved was the second or third such goofy letter received at the precinct the previous year. The others, the rumor went, "were sent to Detective McCan"—the trash can.

Rumor or not, one letter had been filed away and could be retrieved from the Police Property Clerk's Office. The officer picked up the phone and dialed the detectives, who were about to get a look at yet another letter from the poisoned pen of Zodiac.

Chapter 5

THE ZODIAC WILL SPREAD FEAR

SIX months before Joe Proce was shot, on Friday, November 17, 1989, a white prestamped envelope with a ring of stars USA stamp in the upper-right corner arrived amid the pile of morning mail delivered to the 75th Precinct on Sutter Avenue in East New York.

It was addressed to "Anti-Crime," the plainclothes street cops in the Anti-Crime Section of the station house. Drawn on the lower left of the thin envelope was a small circle with a cross on top. An officer opened the envelope and scanned the anonymous letter inside.

The top of the single sheet of paper was dominated by a large circle filled with concentric and radiating lines, like a spider web divided into eleven of the twelve astrological signs. The Taurus section bore the ominous notation "The first sign is dead."

At the center of the web sat "The Zodiac," underlined three times. Curiously, the sign for Virgo the Virgin was omitted from the circle of the doomed. Beneath the web the writer had printed several mysterious sentences, punctuated by large black periods—like bullet holes:

This is the Zodiac. The first sign is dead.
The Zodiac will Kill the twelve signs in the
belt when the Zodiacal light is seen.

The Zodiac will spread fear.
I have seen a lot of police in Jamaica Ave and Eldert
   Lane but
you are not good and will not get the Zodiac. Orion
   is the
one that can stop Zodiac and the Seven Sister.

Zodiac says Orion can stop him. Is "the Seven Sister"
in it with Zodiac, or is she one of the ones who can stop
Zodiac, too? The cryptic, boastful words would later prove
to be strangely accurate. The message was signed "Zodiac" in green ink. At the bottom of the page was a larger
version of the circle-and-cross symbol on the envelope. If
police had checked with experts, they would have found
that Zodiacal light was light reflected from stardust and
was visible in the Northeast in February, March, October,
and November, from 2:00 A.M. until dawn—but they did
not.

The mention of the corner of Jamaica Avenue and Eldert
Lane in the note was an apparent reference to a diner there
frequented by cops, just two short blocks from Proce's
home.

The 75th Precinct was a two-story cinderblock fortress
in the midst of a blighted community from which uniformed officers and plainclothes detectives policed the
neighborhood.

A sign on the wall in the busy second-floor Detective
Squad room read: "Give us 22 minutes, we'll give you a
homicide." The high number of murders in the precinct
was partly the result of business disputes among entrepre-
neurs in the burgeoning crack cocaine industry and partly
the result of more traditional motives, such as hatred, jeal-
ousy, and greed.

When busy cops there received the Zodiac's scrawled
letter threatening an even dozen occult murders, they had
no clues to the identity of the author, which made an investigation of the vague threat almost impossible. It was

hardly the first communication from an EDP, a politically correct acronym for "Emotionally Disturbed Person," which had replaced the term "psycho" in police argot.

Cops checked for any connection to active cases. When nothing was found, the letter was dismissed as probable crank mail. Copies of the letter were passed around the station house as a joke. It was later assigned a serial number and a copy was slipped into an envelope, and sent by departmental mail to the Police Property Clerk's Office at the 84th Precinct on Gold Street in downtown Brooklyn. There, it was vouchered into a log and disappeared into a file cabinet just before Thanksgiving.

As the new decade of the nineties dawned, Zodiac was true to his word. As he had vowed in the letter, he began his work—stalking potential victims on the night streets of East New York, patiently weaving his web.

Chapter 6

LEAD FROM SILVER

AFTER listening carefully to confirm that the neighbors were not at home, and looking out the windows to check for cops, Eddie turned on the stereo in the kitchen. He set it to very loud, thumping music, the kind he hated. He used to like Donny Osmond and the Beatles, but Eddie didn't listen to music anymore. He went back in his room and turned the sound on his TV way up. His half-sister, Chachi, was at school and their mother, Gladys, had gone out into the freezing March sunshine to attend church and go shopping, as usual.

Eddie picked up his new weapon and loaded it. He went a day and a night without sleep or food while he was making the latest gun, using a drill to ream out a barrel from a length of lead pipe. His thin but muscular arms strained as he scraped a long, round file in and out of the metal tube. He carefully assembled the pieces of pipe and a bolt into a breech chamber and firing pin. When he was done, he wrapped the handle and the end of the muzzle with white adhesive tape. His stomach grumbled with hunger, but he could not sleep or rest once he had started making a gun. Not until it was completed and ready for testing.

He had once made the mistake of putting ammunition that was too powerful into one of his pipe pistols, which almost blew up in his hands. The bullet misfired and the thin pipe ballooned but did not explode. It could have been very bad.

He made a target in his room by creating a stack of boxes and books on top of his low dresser. He placed an old phone book on top and leaned it against the wall at the height of someone's head. He wrapped the muzzle of the gun in an old blanket. Looking down the barrel, he aimed at the target's head, the metal tube pointing at a spot just above the black letters of the word BROOKLYN on the front cover of the phone directory.

BOOM!

The twelve-inch pistol-pipe kicked violently in his right hand. In a spray of white paint and plaster, the phone book tumbled off onto the chest and landed with a thump on the floor. A cloud of blue gunsmoke rose up, mushroomed on the ceiling, and vanished. The gun was suddenly hot in his hand.

Excited, grinning with glee, Eddie picked up the book. The 9-millimeter bullet had perforated more than an inch of paper like nothing. It had blasted a hole right through Brooklyn, from "Abbas" to "Zweig," and imbedded itself in the wall. He quickly used his patching kit, slathering spackling compound, tape, and paint over the bullet hole. Then he wiped up the plaster dust, turned off the radio, and checked the windows to make sure he had attracted no attention. He hadn't. It wasn't the first time he had fired one of his guns in the bedroom. The best day of the year for weapons testing was the Fourth of July, with all the fireworks going off and people shooting guns into the air outside. New Year's Eve at midnight was pretty good, too. The previous bullet holes in the wall and ceiling were covered with dried patches of paint, which stood out from the older, surrounding paint job.

Unlike ancient magicians and alchemists, who failed to magically transmute lead into precious metals like gold,

Eddie worked successfully in reverse, turning silver into lead.

Eddie's work did not bring in any money. He had to finance his hobby some other way, so he stuffed plastic bags and strings up into the coin-return slots of busy pay phones on the street. The crude device trapped any coins refunded by the machine and, when he returned days later, Eddie would reap a harvest of quarters, dimes, and nickels and return home with his pockets jingling with silver, which he would stack inside his bureau. The more phones he did, the more he made. It was easy and he was his own boss. In the daylight, he would turn some of the change into bills and some into postal money orders. He used the money orders to buy things through the mail, like magazines, books, videos, knives, and bullets.

He was pleased that the neighborhood financed his work, that East New York funded Zodiac. When you added the seventeen cents per bullet cost, plus more for pipes and materials, it came out to about twenty-five cents per round. One quarter, one shot.

The best part was that he didn't even have to leave his apartment to get ammo, much less leave the city. Eddie loved it when the brown-uniformed United Parcel Service guy delivered the little brown packages to his door. The small, heavy boxes were labeled only with a discreet rectangle that said "ORM-D Small Arms Ammunition." He would sign for them with his real first name and his mother's last name. It was always exciting to hurry into his room, close the door, and open his latest package, especially when it contained fifty rounds of gleaming bullets in neat rows, like soldiers awaiting his orders.

Eddie cleaned his weapon and removed the hot, acrid-smelling brass cartridge left inside. It took him a full thirty seconds to reload the single-shot weapon with one of the cheap, soft-nosed lead bullets meant for target practice.

On that day, Eddie may have continued about the business of his chosen profession seriously. But he may not have been able to resist posing menacingly in front of his mirror, smirking and waving the gun, like Robert DeNiro in *Taxi Driver*. Did he also practice his quick draw and point the deadly dark hole of the barrel at his reflection in the glass?

Each time he made a gun, it took him less time. It still took a lot of effort to craft the pistol from plans in the army manual he got by mail order, but it was better for Eddie that way. If he left the safety of his apartment, he could buy a gun on the corner in no time, if he had enough money. But whoever he bought it from might give him up to the cops as soon as he got into trouble. Eddie hated street people and feared them. You couldn't trust them, they were sinners. Like the Bible said, "Without are dogs, and sorcerers and whoremongers, and murderers, and idolaters, and whosoever loveth and maketh a lie." Besides, he made the mistake of going public with a gun once before, and he wasn't about to repeat that error. Proudly showing off and firing that starter's pistol in class at Franklin K. Lane High School six years before had resulted in his suspension during his junior year. That made him very angry and, after that, he went to school less and less, and one day in 1985 he just stopped going at all. He never graduated but his class picture, of Eddie dressed in a tuxedo, appeared in the 1986 yearbook. Up to that time the most famous alumnus was mobster John Gotti.

He put the pierced phone book target and the old blanket in the back of his closet. Eddie's stuff, from first grade to last week, filled the orderly shelves of the closet as well as the drawers of his chest and bureau.

Certificates of merit for attendance and achievement at PS 159 and his Viewmaster slide viewer were stored neatly next to several porno videos with titles like *Biggies* and *Long Dan Silver*.

Eddie's evolving interests were evident in the neat stacks of books and magazines, which transformed in midstack where *G. I. Joe* comic books stopped and *Soldier of*

Fortune mercenary magazines began. Where *UFO & Outer Space* comics ended, *Guns & Ammo, Handgunner, Firepower*, and survivalist magazines began. Mail-order toy catalogs gave way to mail-order gun catalogs.

His childhood collections of coins and stamps had been superseded by brass knuckles and a knife collection.

A collection of baseball cards dated from the time when Eddie wanted to be a pitcher for the New York Mets. His most recent career choice was reflected by a newer collection of serial killer trading cards, including Ted Bundy, Charles Manson, and Son of Sam David Berkowitz, who had killed people right there in Brooklyn.

Eddie's old toy soldiers were no longer as interesting as the new green surplus military gunbelt with canteen, or the gas masks, the Swiss Army helmet, two blowguns, a crossbow, and a large machete.

The Blackstone's Magic Set box in the corner of the closet had not been opened in years, but Eddie's occult books on how to conjure up the devil were well-thumbed and used often.

Eddie picked up the habit of collecting from his mother, who arrived home in the afternoon, carrying a plastic shopping bag filled with a few food items and household cleaning products. She had also purchased another colorful set of cute matryoshka dolls for her kitchen collection. The egglike nested wooden figurines opened to reveal another, smaller doll inside the first, and then another and another and another. Sometimes, when you thought you had exposed all of the inner selves, there was still one tiny effigy hiding inside.

Carmen Gladys Alvarado was very religious. She took the long subway ride to Manhattan every day to attend the Spanish-language mass at St. Patrick's Cathedral on Fifth Avenue. It made her feel good to attend mass in the magnificent gothic cathedral, and she would pray for ''power'' for her children. After church, she usually did a little shopping before catching the subway home.

Gladys had been a beautiful teenager growing up in Puerto Rico and was still very pretty after four children and three husbands. She looked ten years younger than her forty-four years. Her silky, shoulder-length black hair was parted in the middle. It was coiffed up on top and gathered in the back in a close French braid. She brewed some fresh coffee and poured it into her golden "Gladys" mug on the kitchen table as she put away her purchases.

She had moved into the third-floor walkup at 2730 Pitkin Avenue, between Euclid Avenue and Pine Street, some twenty years earlier, when her brother and other family and friends still lived there. After she was laid off from her job at a Manhattan store, she went on welfare and had been on it ever since. She was the last of the old tenants living in the decaying building.

Two older daughters, Angelica and Cathy, had married and moved out, leaving Gladys with Eddie and her youngest, Gladys Reyes, eleven, whom everyone knew by her nickname, Chachi.

Gladys did not want her kids to end up on drugs or hanging out on the street. She wanted them to be religious, to practice sexual abstinence outside of marriage, to attend church, and, as much as possible, she wanted them to stay in the apartment, a refuge from the drugs and crime and sin outside.

Eddie respected his mother's wishes and stayed in the apartment most of the time. He went out only to go to church, or to run a few errands, or for his late-night walks while Gladys and Chachi were asleep.

He was a happy and outgoing child until he suffered two seizures during a high fever at the age of five. After that, his mother noticed, he became sullen and withdrawn. In junior high school, a teacher told Gladys that she should take her son to a doctor because he would "space out" in the middle of a conversation. But Eddie didn't like going to the doctor and Gladys never took him. Nor did she seek professional help when Eddie, going through puberty, suddenly stopped talking to people and began beating Chachi, who was then only three years old. Instead, Gladys tried in vain to convince her son to seek companionship.

"Why don't you look for a friend and talk to some-body?" she would ask her son.

"I don't want to talk to nobody," Eddie would answer. He would interrupt people who spoke to him, saying, "Why should I talk to you?" Then he would walk away.

Despite the conspicuous porno videos, he was never seen or heard expressing any attraction to girls and he never dated. Once a good student interested in art, math, and science, Eddie's grades went downhill. His school career ended after the gun incident at his high school, which was near Jamaica Avenue and surrounded on three sides by cemeteries. He could have returned after the suspension, but he was so angry, he refused to go back.

If Gladys had any idea what might have caused her son's abrupt personality change, she did not share her suspicions with strangers.

After Eddie left school, army recruiters came to the house because he was eager to be a soldier and yearned to wear a Special Forces green beret. It never happened. Eddie later said he didn't pass a test, but his mother told people he wasn't allowed to go because he was an only son. She may have declined to sign permission for her minor son to enter the armed forces, which might explain why he virtually stopped speaking even to her. A very brief attempt to work with his stepfather, Chachi's dad, at his cabinetry shop was a disaster and the youth retreated to his room. Eddie never spoke to his own father, who was out of his life by the age of three.

After he stopped going to school, Eddie began to act like the man of the house and insisted that no one outside the family be allowed in the apartment. Incredibly, after many violent temper outbursts, that was exactly what happened. The teenager assumed the role of a sullen, unemployed, abusive head of a dysfunctional family.

Gladys simply adjusted and kept out of her son's way as much as possible, which wasn't difficult since he spent most of his waking hours in his room, the larger of the two bedrooms.

But Chachi was Eddie's punching bag and felt betrayed by her mother, who she believed did not protect her from her brother's mistreatment. The abuse of his younger sister began when she was only three and continued for seven years.

At first, Eddie was nice to his cute, dark-haired tomboy sister Chachi, who was named by her elder sister Cathy for her resemblance to the Scott Baio character on the TV sitcom *Happy Days*. Brother and sister would watch wrestling on Eddie's television and he would show her his knife collection and how to use his blowguns and his pellet gun.

But he soon began abusing her whenever they were alone. He would sneak into her room and suffocate her with a pillow for no reason. Once, she ran downstairs to her baby-sitter to escape a beating from Eddie, who was in high school and a karate student. He laughed sadistically and warned her: "If you go down to your baby-sitter, I'm gonna fuck you up tomorrow."

True to his word, the next day, Eddie yanked her hair, punched her, and kicked her severely enough to leave bruises, one of many such assaults.

As she got older the beatings got worse and Chachi began looking for weapons of her own. At PS 159, Chachi hid knives inside books in the school library.

The situation had come to a head the previous year, when Chachi was ten years old. She brought a loaded .22-caliber pistol to her fourth-grade class, telling friends she was going to kill another girl. Authorities began asking questions, such as where did a fourth-grader get a gun?

Eddie stopped beating Chachi around that time, after police had been called to the apartment several times while he was tormenting his sister. He had wanted to be a cop when he was a kid, but he was not happy to see officers from the Seven-Five at his door. The macho man of the house had to back down in front of Chachi and his mother and the neighbors, because he knew if police searched his room he would go to jail.

Oddly enough, Eddie was no longer mad at Chachi. He was mad at the cops—and New York City. It was 1989, not long before the first Zodiac letter arrived at the 75th Precinct.

The city had humiliated him and ruined his life by suspending him from school. Eddie already felt belittled by the cops, even before they made him look bad at home.

Eddie had taken the subway into lower Manhattan and walked to Police Headquarters at One Police Plaza near City Hall. He intended to apply for a gun permit and picked up an application at the Permit Section, but was shocked to learn that the application fee was two hundred dollars. He was ashamed to tell the clerk he didn't have the money, so he left without even filling out the form.

It was a painful and frustrating time for Eddie. He had left school and he couldn't join the army. His full sister, Cathy, whom he was close to, found a husband and moved out. It was no longer safe to beat his little sister.

Without Chachi to torture, he had been slowly filling up with anger and pain and loneliness. He was afraid of his pain and had no place to get rid of it.

On his nightly journeys on the streets of East New York, dressed in black, like a burglar or peeping Tom, Eddie had been searching for a way to get rid of his bad feelings and feel good again.

Inside Eddie's psychology book, in another apparent attempt at self-diagnosis, Eddie had circled a passage on page 509 and underlined the word "voyeurism":

The observation of the genitalia or sexual activity of others—voyeurism (scotophilia) or wearing the clothing of the opposite sex (transvestism) is labeled deviant. Further, to be considered normal, sexual pleasure should be obtainable without inflicting mental or bodily pain (sadism) or being the victim of such pain.

Eddie liked to watch people without getting involved with them, like on TV, whether it was from his window, wandering the streets, or hiding in the dark graveyard.

That night, it was time for Eddie to get down to business. He knew what to do. The California Zodiac had made a strong impression upon him. He particularly liked the 1969 letter the killer wrote to a newspaper that talked of "a kill rampage," and threatened to "cruise around and pick off all street people or cripples that are alone, then move on to kill some more until I have killed over a dozen people." Officially, the original Zodiac killed six and wounded several others, but the mysterious murderer claimed thirty-six victims. He said he was collecting slaves, who would serve him in the afterlife.

It reminded Eddie of a quote from the Book of Job, in which God spoke to Job from out of the whirlwind and gave him a long list of things that mere men were supposed to be unable to do, like "Canst thou bind the sweet influences of Pleiades, or loose the bands of Orion? Canst thou bring forth Mazzaroth [the twelve signs] in his season . . . knowest thou the ordinances of heaven?" Eddie believed Zodiac could bring forth the twelve signs, using the ordinances of heaven. He composed a new message with gloves on and put it in his pocket. He wouldn't need an envelope or a stamp this time.

He waited until well after midnight, when his mother and Chachi were asleep, and checked his astronomical chart for March 8, 1990. The only ones who could stop him, Orion and the Seven Sisters, were not in the sky and his constellation, Leo, was.

It was time. Standing in front of the mirror, Eddie put on a scarf and his maroon Soldier of Fortune commando beret. On the front of the beret was a silver pin of a miniature Special Forces beret with crossed daggers. On the pin was the Omega symbol—the same symbol as his sign, Leo the Lion. Also, Omega stood for the apocalypse in the Bible, in Revelations. Apocalypse now.

He was a warrior and tonight he would test himself in battle for the first time. But before battle, he must pray for protection and success.

He wrote the 83rd Psalm on a piece of pure paper and strung it around his neck to keep him safe in battle and prevent his capture, as prescribed in his Moses book of magic.

Now for the final spell. He would find out if these magic words worked any better than the ones in his old magic set.

He mixed the rose oil and salt into the water bowl and chanted the 20th Psalm seven times before anointing himself with the sweet water.

In stalking man, the most dangerous game, Eddie's challenge was that he was hunting only men and had just one shot at them. In East New York, the prey might have a much better gun than Eddie, a gun full of bullets.

He had several targets that he had been following for weeks. One was an old man with a cane, who walked home from the subway every night, like clockwork. Hopefully, he wouldn't have to wait in the freezing cemetery for too long. Eddie quietly left the dark apartment for his first night on the job.

It was time for him to start a new collection.

Chapter 7

YOU'RE KILLING ME

MARIO dozed off on the long subway ride from his job at a Manhattan restaurant to his home in Brooklyn. It was late and his head nodded, as the motion of the train rocked him into the familiar, unrestful nap aboard the overheated subway car. Mario Orozco, fifty-nine, had been riding the same train home from his job for sixteen years and there was no danger he would sleep past his stop, which he knew in his sleep.

He could have been home safely in bed. After taxes, his union-wage kitchen job paid him less than he could have collected on disability and welfare. Mario had been born sickly and blind. Injections restored the sight in one eye but left him partially crippled in one leg. As a result, he walked with a cane and a limp, but he always stood on his own two feet. He was a proud man and would have nothing to do with welfare.

He was born in Medellín, Colombia, where he had left his common-law wife, Maria, and their two children, a twenty-three-year-old boy and a girl, twenty-five. Six months previously, he had been back for one of his periodic visits to his homeland to visit his family and see his two grandchildren.

Despite his handicaps, Mario had always worked. Despite medical problems, the grueling hours, and the long commute at night, he was warm-hearted and well-liked by his coworkers. The laugh lines etched into his friendly face showed Mario liked a good joke.

When the subway jerked to a stop in East New York, it was 1:45 A.M., March 8, 1990. Mario pushed himself up from the plastic bench with the carved wooden cane given him by a friend and moved out the door. Yawning, not yet awake, the cold air outside soon woke him up. His breath fogged in the sub-freezing early-morning air. He helped himself down the stairs of the elevated platform using the stair rail and began limping the ten blocks to the modest home he owned with his sister on Forbell Street, just south of Atlantic Avenue.

It was dark and quiet in the nearby cemetery, with its unmoving monuments, vaults, and marble statues of draped urns and angels. One motionless gargoyle was wearing a maroon beret—with a glinting pin, bearing a small Greek letter omega.

The handsome, unshaven gargoyle suddenly smirked and began to move toward Jamaica Avenue. He had seen a familiar face, and a familiar limp, out in the land of the living.

Zodiac.

Mario did not look up at the clear, cold night sky. He did not have time for hobbies like astronomy and had no idea what astrological sign he was. He kept his eyes on the sidewalk and bundled his coat collar up around his lean, wrinkled face, against the biting, twenty-five-degree air. He did not notice a young man in dark clothing behind him, on the other side of Nichols Avenue, shadowing him on the otherwise-empty block.

Just before Mario reached Atlantic Avenue, the man crossed the street on his blind side and came up behind him.

Bang!

Mario, a Scorpio, felt a hot sting in his back.

"You're killing me! Help!" he screamed. The sidewalk

seemed to fly up and slam into Mario's side.

As he lay there, the gunman casually stepped over him, straddling him, and pointed the barrel of the gun straight at Mario's head. He thought he was going to die. He froze and closed his eyes but nothing happened. Holding his breath, squinting through closed lids, he peeked at the gunman above him in the dim streetlight.

The barrel of the gun looked huge and close in the man's hands, which were covered with black leather gloves. A dark hat and a scarf hid most of his mute face, like an executioner.

The shooter stood over him for what seemed to Mario like a full two minutes. He was praying to God that the guy would not pull the trigger again, that he would think Mario was dead. Why didn't anybody come out of the houses, just a few yards away, to help him? Why didn't somebody call the police?

It was East New York.

Suddenly, the masked gunman wasn't there. Mario did not see the man wrap a paper note around the gun and place them both on the pavement nearby.

Mario waited. Then he cautiously lifted his head in time to see his attacker moving westward on the far side of Atlantic Avenue in an ungainly sprint. When he was out of sight, Mario pulled himself up and resumed his walk home. No one came out to help him. He had the same drowsy feeling he had on the train, as if he were sleepwalking.

Every night there were people hanging around on Atlantic, street people, druggies looking for or selling drugs, hookers hooking customers, but they were nowhere to be seen.

Zodiac's shot had temporarily cleared the streets.

Mario saw a car slow down and glide by, but he didn't try to flag it down. After all, he was walking, how badly could he be hurt? A man didn't die on his feet. It seemed to take a very long time for him to shuffle the four blocks to his house and let himself in.

He removed his jacket and felt his back. His cold hand came back hot and bloody. Still standing, the restaurant worker washed the blood off his hand and put on a pot of coffee in his small kitchen, which made him feel better. Dead men don't make coffee. Then he picked up the wall phone and dialed 911.

"I've been shot," he said into the phone, as his coffee bubbled.

The bullet had lodged next to Mario's spine, between two spinal discs, but it did not paralyze him. Doctors at Jamaica Hospital had to leave the slug where it was, because an operation to remove it could itself result in paralysis.

Mario was afraid. Why would anyone want to kill him? The guy didn't even try to rob him. He just wanted him dead. He had to be crazy, and, if he was crazy, he might try again.

The victim told the detectives who interviewed him in his hospital bed what had happened.

The police found nothing at the scene. They had no bullet for comparison, no witnesses, no identification, no case.

All they had was Mario, who surprised the investigators by telling them that the shooter could have been a Spanish guy, but he believed it was a white guy, about twenty-five years old, with blond hair.

One of the detectives asked him how he could possibly know that, since the gunman's face and hands were covered and he did not speak.

"He ran like a white boy," Mario answered and gave a smile.

Chapter 8

KILLING TIME

AFTER a few days, Eddie relaxed and realized the cops were not going to show up at the door.

How could they? There were no fingerprints on the gun or the note. But he began to regret leaving the weapon. It took a long time to build, and cost money. Also, maybe there was some way they could tell where he bought the pipes? But why wasn't there anything about the dead target in the papers or on TV? The cops must be keeping it quiet because they don't know anything.

When Eddie found a documentary on TV about a serial killer, like Zodiac or Ted Bundy, he would watch it, study it, and take notes. For him, the shows were educational, like his personal library on the same subject. He learned how serial killers worked, how they killed, and how they got caught. Some had bad luck and others got caught because they took souvenirs from their victims. Eddie knew that. That's why he took nothing from the old man.

During a documentary on Ted Bundy, he made a note that Ted raped and killed as many as forty women.

Wow, thought Eddie, filled with admiration as snapshots of the pretty corpses flashed on the screen.

Look how many victims he has. I'm going to try and get as many as him.

But his favorite, his idol, was Zodiac.

Zodiac, thought Eddie, *spread fear. He was in control and held a city in fear for quite awhile, and never got caught.*

Gladys didn't think it strange for her grown son to be taking notes about infamous murderers and placing them in files and notebooks.

She noted it with an indulgent smile. It was nothing new, he had been doing it for several years. Anything about war fascinated him. At least he wasn't a drug dealer on the street.

Every day, Eddie read the Bible aloud in his room, praying and talking to himself for hours and hours. Sometimes the conversations became quite loud and animated. Eddie ranted and muttered and spat out obscenities, as if he were arguing with someone else in the empty room.

When the spirit moved him, he would emerge from his domain with open Bible and preach through the house, delivering fire-and-brimstone sermons to his mother as she cleaned the kitchen. An exasperated Gladys interrupted her son:

"Why don't you put down the Bible and go out and get a job?"

He snapped out of it, startled.

"It's not time for me to get a job," he replied, with a sneer.

Eddie was amused. His mother did not know he already had a job.

He passed the time before his next mission by praying, reading, and watching television, as usual. He loved to watch horror movies, especially *The Exorcist* and Freddy Krueger movies.

His favorite magazine was *Soldier of Fortune*. He had their logo pin, which was a mercenary soldier's beret with an omega symbol, which also symbolized Eddie's sign, Leo the Lion. Behind the beret were bayonets, overlapped in a cross.

In that month's issue, there was an interesting article.

"Drug War Firefight—U.S. Army Rangers Take on Crack Gangs in Tacoma," about a mercenary soldier who came home and got into a big war with the drug dealers who had infested his block.

Eddie marked every day that passed on his Catholic church wall calendar, on which he had neatly inked all the Jewish holy days of the year.

He consulted the star chart and soon it was time. After his mother and Chachi were asleep, he prepared another note and another gun and then dressed and completed his secret prayer rituals.

Eleven signs to go. He must keep on going. On the way out of the apartment, Eddie synchronized his black digital commando watch with the silly hobo clown clock on the kitchen counter, which read just past midnight, Thursday, March 29, 1990.

Time for the Second Sign.

Chapter 9

GOD WAS WITH ME

GERMÁN lurched unsteadily down the sidewalk under the elevated subway line on Jamaica Avenue, clutching a half-finished quart of malt liquor in one hand. It was not his first of the evening, nor his second, but it would be his last.

He had come to the U.S. from his native Ecuador in 1983 and worked five days a week in a lamp factory elsewhere in Brooklyn.

After work, he usually took the subway to the rented apartment he shared with his girlfriend in the Bronx. But on that night, March 29, 1990, the husky factory worker had had a fight with his girlfriend at a party.

Germán Montenedro, thirty-four, was completely drunk.

Dressed in a heavy black coat, he had taken the subway to East New York, intending to stay at his father's house on Nichols Avenue, but he was indecisive.

Germán decided to go home and started up the stairs to take the train back to the Bronx.

He tripped on one of the stairs halfway up, and stopped to take a long swallow of the golden liquid, which the frosty, 35-degree air kept decently chilled. He muttered, took another drink, and seemed to change his mind. Then he turned around and started back down the stairs with the exaggerated and deliberate caution of the intoxicated.

From the empty stadium bleachers on the athletic field of nearby Franklin K. Lane High School, a lone figure, dressed in black and invisible in the dark, silently watched Germán's progress with growing interest.

Zodiac.

As Germán staggered west, weaving and drinking, the figure vanished from the bleachers and appeared on the street behind him. The tipsy target walked very slowly past the cemeteries, which gave his pursuer time to think.

The drunk looked familiar but was not one of his intended targets. He did not know his sign.

But the time was right and none of the other targets was out in the cold that night.

It was too cloudy to see that Leo the Lion was in the sky and Orion and the Seven Sisters were not. It was an open window of opportunity.

Here was a sinner under his gun. But what if this guy was the same sign as the old guy down by Atlantic? Should he take a chance?

After four blocks, the target emptied the bottle of alcohol at August Avenue, then tossed it aside.

He swayed to the southern side of the avenue and turned around again, heading east at a faster pace.

It looked like he had wanted to finish the bottle before going on the subway or somewhere else. It had to be somewhere else, because, after two more blocks, he veered away from the subway and went south onto Nichols Avenue, where twenty-one days before the old man had been shot—just four blocks away.

It was a sign.

Zodiac looked around, made his decision, and moved in. He pulled out his weapon. As he took aim, the target started to turn to the left, toward him. He had to shoot.

Bang!

Germán felt like he had been clubbed over the head and was unconscious when he hit the pavement.

Zodiac bent over the unmoving target and quickly felt

his pockets. He found cash in one pocket and left it. Zodiac was not a thief. Another pocket held keys and a passport. He took the document and ran south on Nichols.

When he was out of sight and a safe distance away, Zodiac stopped for a time check on his digital watch. It was 2:57 A.M. He opened the passport. He had to get rid of it quickly. The date of birth listed on the Ecuadoran passport was "28 Mai 1955." He was a different sign. He was a Gemini. The Second Sign. Good.

God was with him.

And the target's first name was Germán, like the country. Faust was German. Another sign.

Zodiac changed hats, and, as he walked quickly past a trash can, casually tossed the passport inside with a gloved hand. He didn't keep trophies.

Germán woke up in a nightmare. He was cold and lying on a sidewalk in a pool of his own blood. His left side was wet with blood.

The 9-millimeter bullet had entered his left side, near the bottom of his ribcage, and it had ripped through his liver. The slug had continued almost completely through his chest and had lodged just under the skin on his lower right side.

Germán only knew he was bleeding and in pain. He thought he had been shot. He scrambled to his feet and realized he was on his corner. He could see his father's sandstone town house, with its curved bay window, on the left side of the street, only forty meters away.

He immediately fell on his face. God be with me, he prayed, before struggling to his feet again. He walked several more steps but was too dizzy to stay up and fell again. He was in shock and still drunk. It took him two more attempts before he fell onto the front stoop, rang the bell, and began moaning for help.

Germán was terrified. Why did somebody shoot him for nothing? He must be crazy or drugged up.

When a Spanish translator in the Brookdale Hospital emergency room told Germán that the doctors had said he was going to survive, he thought it was a miracle.

''God was with me,'' he said.

Chapter 10

RISING STAR

EDDIE was angry. It was Tuesday, June 19, 1990—fifteen days since he sent his letter to The *Post*, and another identical one to *60 Minutes*, after shooting his third target, and nothing had happened. Where were the stories? Where was the fear? Maybe they were as lazy as the cops.

Eddie opened his Moses magic book to page 135, to remind himself what he had acquired. Under ''What Man May Obtain From The Twelve Signs,'' he looked up the astrological signs he had accumulated.

The First Sign in his collection was the old man with the cane near Atlantic, a Scorpio. The book said that ''In the Scorpion, the angels have power over suffering and terror, over which man makes against God, over common privileges. They compel the conscience to obedience and also force devils to keep their agreements with men, and vice versa.'' With that sign, Eddie's deal with the devil was sealed in blood. Both he and the devil had to honor the bargain.

The Second Sign was the stumbling drunk, the Gemini. The book said that the Twins governed bodily changes and travel and caused love between brethren, friends and neighbors, ''and give warning against dangers, persons and objects.'' Good.

The Third Sign, the last one, was the old man with the

cane in front of his house, Taurus the Bull, through which "all transactions and enterprises are prospered and fostered, so that they may go forward with the will of God, but to this end constant prayers are necessary, and particularly on Sunday." Eddie was compelled to keep his part of the bargain, but why wasn't it working? Something was wrong.

Eddie went out for a walk but never made it past the newsstand. From a stack of *New York Post*s, the word ZODIAC leaped up at him. The Zodiac letter was on the front page. He reached into his pocket for change, quickly bought a copy, and rushed back home.

At last, it had hit the papers, he thought with a grin, as he opened the newspaper, sitting on the bed in his room. At last, he was getting attention.

He liked the front-page headline, "Riddle of the Zodiac Shooter." Eddie was the only one in the city who knew the answer to the riddle. He was in control.

Excited, he turned to page seven and began to read. "Police Probing Zodiac Shooter" was at the top of the page, above some picture of Mayor David Dinkins and Jacqueline Onassis. Zodiac was a star, too.

"Police are investigating whether three shootings, at first believed unrelated, are connected to a bizarre letter sent to the *Post*—with the signature 'Zodiac.' "

He stopped short when he reached the last sentence in the seventh paragraph: "None of the victims died." He stood up.

None of the victims died? No! How? Zodiac shot them. They fell and didn't move. How could they not be dead? Eddie felt the anger flowing, as he continued to read. The cops also said the Zodiac letter "does not appear similar" to any of the San Francisco Zodiac letters.

Not similar? No. They had to believe there was only one Zodiac! Eddie was beginning to lose control, pacing back and forth across the shining blue floor.

Wait. Eddie stopped pacing.

Maybe they were lying, trying to trick him into doing something stupid, like striking when conditions, or the stars, were not right? Maybe they thought they could make him pick up the telephone and dial one of the numbers at the end of the story—so they could trace the call and catch him? He would not do that. He would only strike when heavenly and earthly conditions were good, like tomorrow night.

He had to stay in control in order to become the master of all things.

Not dead. It made Zodiac look bad. Did that mean that he had not fulfilled his part of the bargain? Either way, he had no choice. He had to keep on going.

The next day, June 20, Zodiac was already off the front page of the *Post* and had been replaced by a big picture of Nelson Mandela, who was visiting New York.

But all of page three was about Zodiac. The big headline was "ZODIAC DRAGNET, Detectives Form Task Force to Locate Shooter." A whole task force for Zodiac. If Zodiac was so important, why wasn't it on the front page?

Below the top story was a big picture of the old man with the cane on 87th Road, and a second story, "Latest Victim Warns of Heartless Gunman." Heartless gunman. Yes. Eddie was proud he had passed the test of battle, that he could be so cold, that he had what it took to get the job done, to carry out the mission.

In the picture, the old man was in a hospital bed, in a nightgown, with tubes coming out of his nose. He was alive; it wasn't a lie. And, he had seen Zodiac. It gave Eddie a lot of anger to see him alive. For any of them to have survived.

He was happy to read that the gunman was described as a heavyset black man with a mustache. His disguise had worked. So had the magic.

At the bottom of the page was a third story, "Stargazers

Say Madman Will Strike Again.'' Well, they got one thing right. It was time for the Fourth Sign.

Tonight.

Zodiac will get more attention. Zodiac will be back on the front page soon. But first Eddie carefully cut the page free and inserted it in the Zodiac scrapbook he had begun with yesterday's front-page story.

He washed his hands, put on his gloves, took out his writing supplies, and crafted two more messages for the next mission. One he would leave near the target. The other he would place in one of the star envelopes, which he addressed to the *Post*. He left space on both to add the time and place and sign.

Eddie had been upset that the *Post* story the day before said it was not the same Zodiac as San Francisco. He got the big dictionary out of his closet and opened it to the foreign phrases section in the back. He copied two impressive sayings, one in French, the other in Latin, onto the new messages.

He also added ''Faust'' with a new cross symbol coming out of the bottom of the underlined name of the magician. At each of three ends of the cross was a number *6*.

Then he made a little drawing on the message to the *Post* that he was sure would convince them there was only one Zodiac.

After his usual preparatory ritual of prayers and ablutions, Eddie left his apartment and went to work hours earlier than usual. He cautiously reconnoitered on the edge of his target zone but saw cops everywhere, part of the Zodiac dragnet. They were grabbing black guys, frisking them, checking ID, and letting them go.

They were looking for Zodiac, but they wouldn't find him in Brooklyn tonight. Eddie had to smile to himself as he boarded a subway for Manhattan. It was funny.

The only problem was timing. Because of all the cops in the neighborhood, he couldn't hit one of the targets he knew. He had to find a new one, which could take hours.

He had to hurry to find a target, before Leo the Lion set or Orion and the Seven Sisters rose into the humid night sky. Time for the Fourth Sign.

Time to increase the fear.

Chapter 11

TRACKING ZODIAC

OCCASIONALLY, a newspaper cliché, like a gunman holding a city hostage, came true. With Zodiac, the nightmare came true twice—once on each coast.

The original Zodiac inspired the first *Dirty Harry* movie starring Clint Eastwood, who chased "Scorpio," a giggling sicko who loved to machine-gun innocent victims. The Hollywood incarnation of Zodiac obligingly made Inspector Harry Callahan's day, and was blown away by a single blast from Clint's giant .44 Magnum pistol. In reality, the Bay Area Zodiac was never caught.

"I like killing people," exulted one Zodiac letter.

Zodiac said he believed his victims magically became his slaves and would be waiting to do his bidding in the afterlife, something that gave the public gooseflesh and drove detectives to their breaking points.

Both Zodiacs had several things in common: they loved generating mass fear with creepy occult threats, they loved taunting police in the newspapers, and they both had a bloodlust to hunt and kill human beings that was stronger than—or in place of—their sex drive.

When the New York Zodiac Killer made, or rather borrowed, a name for himself, he inspired terror among New Yorkers, who—like the citizens of San Francisco two decades earlier—had a new reason to fear the night.

When the Zodiac letter arrived at the *Post*, I was a dayside street reporter who, along with every other reporter in town, thought it was a hell of a story and wanted to get in on it.

Twelve years earlier, I had started out as a copyboy and worked my way up to reporter, spending years on the street covering police stories, including literally thousands of murders, shoot-outs, robberies, and other crimes. One of my first assignments as a cub reporter was the Brooklyn sentencing of convicted Son of Sam killer David Berkowitz. The surreal scene of a robed judge on the bench discussing demons and their advice with the deranged, pasty-faced postal worker was unforgettable. Crime and serial killers had always been a fascination for me and the walls of my home were covered with pulp fiction art and bookshelves containing a large collection of true-crime books as well as first editions of hardboiled murder mysteries. One of the true-crime books in my collection was *Zodiac*, by Robert Graysmith.

My Irish cop face, surrounded by light brown hair and beard, had many times kept me out of trouble in dangerous situations. In the middle of a riot, I was surrounded by youths with pipes and lumber in their hands.

"You a cop, man?" one of them asked.

"Do I look like a cop?" I asked, putting my hands into the pockets of my London Fog topcoat.

"Yeah, you do," he responded. A hole opened in the ring and I walked through it.

Dressed in a suit and wearing prescription sunglasses year-round, I would arrive at a crime scene, often as the sun came up. With the advantage of daylight, I would look for evidence cops sometimes missed in the dark.

Over the years, I found dozens of shell casings, bullets, and other evidence and turned them over to the police. At the Brooklyn scene of the rubout of Gus Farace, I found one slug and a pair of bloody wraparound shades the murderer of a DEA agent had been wearing when he was himself shot to death. Tracing the route a getaway car took after a drug killing in Queens, I found a blood-spattered murder gun and a bloody scarf discarded by the killers.

Sometimes the violence got too close. Once, working alone, I was held hostage at knife-point by the relative of someone arrested for shooting a woman to death. After almost twenty minutes with a large serrated knife pointed at my ribs, I was able to talk my way out. I got the story, but from that point on I never conducted any interviews with cutlery in sight.

The day the first Zodiac story broke in the paper, it was "the Wood"—the front-page story heralded in type so large that in the old "cold type" days the letters had been carved from wood, not metal.

I started my day at 6:00 A.M., parking my car in front of the six-story sandstone *New York Post* building at 210 South Street on the Lower East Side. On the waterfront, in between Chinatown and the elevated East River Drive, the building had a spectacular view of the river, framed by the Brooklyn Bridge on the right and the Manhattan Bridge on the left.

Only a police reporter could look at such a beautiful sight and think of death and all the people who died trying to swim in the turbulent water. It was spring, time for the warming, roiling waters to give up its dead—all the bodies that had jumped, fallen, or were dumped into it over the winter. Sometimes the "floaters" would compete with fresh corpses for space in the paper.

An eighteen-wheel tanker truck was pumping thousands of gallons of black ink into the side of the rectangular building, as if it were filling up a giant printing press, which it was.

As I entered the building, several laughing pressmen, wearing ink-smeared coveralls and square folded newspaper hats, were leaving. Outside, the nostrils fought with an intriguing mixture of brine and sewage, but inside it smelled like a newspaper—that crisp smell of hot, dry paper and wet ink on top of old oiled machinery.

The *Post*, founded in 1801 by Alexander Hamilton, was the oldest continuously published daily affront to pomposity in America, and, like its founding father, "Alex," on the masthead, was always irritating or dueling with someone.

The elevator took me to the fourth floor and I walked into an almost empty City Room. Deputy Photo Editor Vern Shibla was hard at work, listening to the squawking police radios and speaking on two phones at once, dispatching photographers around the city. He already had home addresses for all three Zodiac victims.

Morning Assignment Editor Maralyn Matlick, my boss at the city desk, sent me out to East New York to talk to the neighbors of Joe Proce, who was still in the hospital, and find victims Mario Orozco and Germán Montenedro.

"Exclusive interviews with the victims would be nice." She laughed as I walked out.

Driving over the rutted, cracked, and potholed streets of Brooklyn reminded me that the name *Brooklyn* itself dated from colonial times and came from a Dutch word meaning "broken land."

Germán Montenedro had been released from the hospital, but he wasn't at home recuperating; he had returned to work. A relative told me where Germán worked and I found him there.

Accompanied by a friend to translate for him, Germán emerged from the lamp factory in a black windbreaker and a black knit cap atop his round, pleasant face. We shook hands. He apologized for the work dirt on his beefy hand.

To escape the din of the factory, we left the open loading dock and walked across the street and talked in front of a vacant lot, which was strewn with garbage and scrap metal.

"Thank God I'm alive! The doctors said I'm very lucky to still be here," said Montenedro, who was still afraid of the gunman he now knew called himself Zodiac. He asked his name not be used while Zodiac was still at large.

"He should turn himself in, before he kills somebody or somebody kills him. What he did was crazy, but God was with me," said Germán nervously, his eyes moving, looking around, as if he thought someone might sneak up on him again.

The young man pulled up his shirt and showed me the healing wound on his left side, which seemed to bring on a rush of remembered emotion.

"When I woke up, there was blood on my side." His eyes were haunted when he described staggering and falling, over and over, thinking he was dying.

Suddenly, Germán said he had to get back to work. He thanked me, shook my hand, and walked away.

"The doctors said it was a miracle he's still alive," his friend said, by way of explanation.

I called the city desk to file my story for the next day's paper, and told Matlick that I had an exclusive interview with a victim, as ordered.

"Only one?" Matlick joked.

She told me that the *Post* was having a good day, that one of my colleagues, reporter Chris Oliver, was sent to Jamaica Hospital and also got an exclusive interview, his with Joe Proce.

A photographer with Oliver snapped Joe's picture in his hospital bed. Joe seemed shaken by the attack, almost three weeks later. He was pale and weak, but not too weak to curse out his assailant. His curses, of course, would not make the paper.

"I want everybody to know that if you get caught by this guy, you haven't got a chance. He strikes without warning," said Joe.

The next day, I got another exclusive interview, this time with the first victim, Mario Orozco; we talked over a cup of delicious coffee in his kitchen.

I knocked on the front door of Mario's small two-story

green and white home on Forbell Street. The door opened a crack and a dark-haired man with a weathered face, prominent nose, and kindly eyes looked out at me. I told him who I was, showed him my press card, and was invited in. I followed Mario through a closed porch and a hallway, as he slowly limped, aided by his cane, to the neat kitchen at the rear of the first floor. He invited me to sit next to him at the small kitchenette table. Mario seemed like a nice guy, but, out of habit, I glanced around and saw no knives in sight.

"I now have an American souvenir to carry with me for the rest of my life," said Mario with a smile, gesturing to where Zodiac's slug was wedged against his spinal column.

I asked Mario why he made a pot of coffee before calling for help.

"It made me feel good" was his answer. As we drank our strong coffee, Mario said, yes, he was still afraid for his life, fearful the gunman "might come back."

He was also bitter that no one called police or tried to help him when he was shot. He was convinced that the white people who lived on the block where he was shot had failed to help him because he was Latino.

"They don't call the cops because they think 'It's only a Spanish dying, that's okay.' "

I responded that some New Yorkers "were afraid to get involved with anything" and that their fearful indifference transcended race, creed, or color. I told him the story of Kitty Genovese, the young white woman who was slowly stabbed to death in 1964 while her white neighbors in Kew Gardens, Queens, ignored her screams and failed to call the police.

The grandfather shook his head in disgust at the tale. He had been in his hometown of Medellín, Colombia, when Genovese was murdered. He found it ironic that he had emerged unscathed from his hometown of Medellín, a hotbed of cocaine carnage, only to be shot on a quiet Brooklyn street nineteen years later.

"I was there for most of my life and nothing ever happened to me. I came here and I almost died. God was with me that night," he said. Mario wanted me to know that he was a hard-working guy and had nothing to do with drugs. In fact, he had to get ready for work soon.

"You went back to work already?" I asked.

"Oh, yes."

"How do you get to and from work now?" I asked, assuming he no longer took the train.

"Subway," he said.

"You still take the train and walk home at night alone?" I asked incredulously.

"Yes, but don't say that in the paper," he said.

"Okay, but aren't you afraid that he's still out there, that he might try again?"

Mario sighed and shrugged. "Yes . . . but I've got to work. Anyway, maybe he knows where I live." He shook my hand and showed me to the door.

"This guy has got to be crazy," he said sadly.

I was the only one on the *Post* staff who had read the *Zodiac* book and it was obvious to me from the start that the East New York shooter was a copycat using the original Zodiac case, and probably the Graysmith book itself, as his guide.

The crude Frankenstein printing, the Zodiac symbol, the phrase "This is the Zodiac," the box score of victims, and the use of the outdated "pigs" to refer to police were all features of the original Zodiac letters. Unlike the original, there was no secret code and no one was dead yet, but the vow to kill one victim for each astrological sign was a new wrinkle.

So far, the Zodiac shooter was oh-for-three. He was batting zero, but the game had just started.

That night, I excitedly told my wife, Riki, a high-school art teacher and artist, about Zodiac. I said it was "a great story," which triggered a running joke of ours, in which Riki pointed out that being a reporter had skewed my outlook on life.

"No," she responded, as if to a slow child, "not good. Bad. People getting shot by a lunatic is bad."

"Yeah, yeah. It's still a great story," I said.

God help me, I loved it.

Chapter 12

THE FOURTH SIGN

LARRY walked slowly past the glittering, gilded West 59th Street entrance to the Plaza Hotel, across the street from the scenic, 843 acres of Central Park, which looked like an impressionist painting in the evening haze. Over the din of traffic on Central Park South, he could barely hear the tinkle of piano music from inside, as people in gowns and tuxedos got in and out of cabs and limousines at the curb. Larry loved piano music, especially piano and flute music.

He was feeling pretty good because he had just gotten a job and would start work the next day. Originally from Brooklyn, he had clear, light black skin and sported a full, droopy black mustache and goatee. He was wearing tan denim pants, a black polo shirt with red horizontal stripes, and a black windbreaker. He was not dressed for the Plaza.

In fact, Larry Parham, thirty, had been wearing the same clothes for several days. He was homeless and was about to make his bed, not in a Plaza suite, but on a park bench. Walking into the park carrying a black bag, the slim six-foot-one-inch man took long, easy strides.

He walked north to the Bethesda Fountain and sat down to rest. Larry was very neat and didn't like wearing dirty clothes or being homeless. He didn't like homeless shelters, either. They were too dangerous. He had even worked in a Brooklyn shelter for awhile, but it didn't work out.

Neither did living with a male roommate in an apartment in Bed-Stuy, because they had begun to argue. Since he broke up with his girlfriend, staying in the park was a way to save money. He had been on welfare until several months before, but wanted his own apartment and was saving up to get a new start. He had already put more than four thousand dollars in the bank.

Larry carried most of his belongings with him in his bag. In his jacket, he carried his Bible, pens, a hairbrush, three contest coupons from a fast-food chain, and, like Joe Proce, a small notebook with religious and personal musings.

He also used the notebook as a memo pad and occasional diary. One page bore a self-admonition, ''don't make the same mistake twice you must learn. Lord help me.''

At the top of that page, which also bore an address, Larry wrote, ''It's a matter of life or death'' next to a cross, that had circles numbered one through four at the ends of the four axes.

Larry was very religious. He attended church every Sunday and always carried a New Testament. He had a drink now and then, but he didn't do drugs. He was troubled and had problems, including a minor arrest record.

About a half an hour after midnight, a bunch of white kids arrived at the fountain area and began partying and playing a radio too loudly for anyone to get any sleep. Larry picked up his stuff and walked south, past the bandshell and down a dark, quiet path.

He found an empty bench in the deserted spot and spread his flattened cardboard over the wooden slats of the bench.

Not far away in the dark, another religious young man watched Parham as he laid out his cardboard bed with the black bag on top, removed a blue pillow from the bag, removed his sneakers, put something inside one of them, and placed the footwear under the bench.

Zodiac.

Parham settled onto his right side, pulled his jacket over his head to stave off the damp, sixty-five-degree air, and went to sleep.

At about 1:45 A.M., an Emergency Medical Service ambulance, a large, square white truck called a "bus," was cruising through the park with two green-uniformed EMS paramedics inside.

Driving down the wide, bench-lined path, the driver, paramedic Edward Tudor*, saw a well-dressed man who looked out of place, sitting on a bench on the left side of the path.

The man was sitting alone on the bench, and had a good view of another bench not too far away, on which a homeless man was asleep. He had an attaché case or bag resting atop the bench, on his left side, the side toward the sleeping man. He was white or Hispanic, with dark, medium-length curly hair that was pushed back behind the ears. He had arched eyebrows and his hairline came together in a widow's peak above his forehead. He seemed to have a light mustache.

The well-dressed man, clad in a gray sport jacket, an open, light-colored shirt, and dark pants and shoes, caught Tudor's attention because he did not seem to belong. He definitely did not look like one of the usual denizens of the nighttime park. At that time of the night, virtually the only civilians in the park were homeless people, hookers, hustlers, and criminal predators.

What's wrong with this picture? Tudor thought to himself. As he drove on toward the bandshell, Tudor passed the sleeping man, who lay motionless on a bench on the right. He continued on past the bandshell and out of sight.

Two hours later, Zodiac crept up on the target in the dim haze. He slowly, carefully reached for one of the sneakers under the bench and removed the object he had seen the target place inside. It was a wallet, as he suspected. Good. Zodiac quietly opened it and threw a tiny beam from his little penlight inside. The wallet held forty-nine dollars in cash, which Zodiac ignored.

In the sky above, unseen through the haze, Zodiac's protector, Leo the Lion, had wandered below the horizon. The Seven Sisters had begun rising from the eastern horizon and were just beginning to peek over the skyscrapers to the east of the park.

Zodiac took off his black leather gloves to remove the thin cards from Larry's billfold, which contained at least ten different pieces of identification, half of which clearly displayed the date of birth of Parham, Larry, as 6/29/59.

He was a Cancer. A different sign. Good. The Fourth Sign.

Zodiac turned off the light, replaced the cards, closed the wallet, and quietly returned it to the sneaker. Zodiac was not a thief.

He withdrew from the bench and, still without his gloves, took out his folded note. He held the paper by the edges, trying not to leave fingerprints. Using his small flashlight again, Zodiac drew two little baseballs—the symbols for Cancer the Crab—in the proper spots on the message he intended to leave. He would fill in the same signs on the letter to the *Post* later and mail it from Brooklyn.

Zodiac refolded his completed message and got ready, putting his gloves back on. He quietly returned to the target bench and placed the note on it, placing a rock on top, so it would not blow away. He was committed. He looked at his watch and noted the time, 3:52 A.M.

He moved in close, brought the gun out, and pointed it down at the sleeping target, about a foot away from the chest. He aimed for the heart.

Bang!

The flash of the shot in the dark lit up the target like a flashbulb, producing an eerie halo in the haze, like holy fire.

The sharp smell of powder was mixed with that of

singed plastic, where Parham's windbreaker had been seared by the muzzle blast and powder burns.

The .38-caliber slug punctured the middle of Parham's chest and barely missed the aorta, the major artery out of the heart. It exited from his body through his right armpit and bored into the wood of the bench.

Larry heard a loud noise and felt pain. He opened his eyes. It was dark. He was in the park and his chest was burning. Something was burning, he could smell it.

He was wet. he pulled the jacket off his head and realized he was covered with blood. He tried to stand up but couldn't. He thought he heard someone in the bushes behind the bench, but he couldn't see anyone. He had to get away. Larry rolled off the bench onto the pavement and started to crawl toward the roadway in the distance.

"Help . . . help me . . ." he said, hardly loud enough to hear himself. Using the jacket, he tried to stop the blood that seemed to be everywhere. He began fading in and out of consciousness.

He tried to walk and call for help but couldn't. He was getting weaker and couldn't stay awake.

Sometime later, the park was brightening with silvery light, the sun was coming up. Larry waved to some guy.

"What's the matter, man?"

Somebody was talking to him. Larry looked up from the ground, where he was crawling on all fours. The guy he waved to was another homeless man, carrying a box of cans and bottles.

"I was shot. I've been hit. I've been hit," Parham said. "Where?"

"My stomach."

The man almost stepped in a puddle of sticky blood. He said something and ran away. Who was that? Was it the guy who Larry had talked to a few days ago, who asked so many questions? He couldn't remember.

Larry had been crawling in circles for over an hour and he was tired. He fell over onto his side into a pool of his own blood and curled up into a fetal position. He was very sleepy.

Police Officer Matthew Micozzi and his partner Robert Calhoun, from the Central Park Precinct, were driving through the park in an unmarked car at sunrise, 5:25 A.M., when they were flagged down by the homeless man who had just seen Larry bleeding and crawling on all fours.

The cops called it in on their radio, requested that an ambulance respond also, and drove over to the bandshell area, where they found Larry lying on his left side, curled up in a ball.

"I was asleep," explained Larry, who was gasping for breath. "I woke up and felt pain. I was bleeding . . . I crawled away . . ."

Calhoun asked the man what his name was.

"Larry . . ."

"The ambulance is coming. Do you have any ID?"

"In my sneaker . . ."

In the growing light, Calhoun located the wallet in the sneaker. It held a little cash and lots of identification, including a motorcycle license and welfare and Medicaid cards.

He also noticed a folded, white piece of paper on the bench, held down by a rock.

On the outside of the note, Calhoun could make out a green circle with a green cross over it. It was the crosshairs symbol he had seen in the *Post*. The Zodiac symbol.

The morning mist had settled on the paper and the green Zodiac symbol was starting to bleed.

An ambulance arrived and the paramedics began to strip Larry and bandage him, inserting an intravenous line and bag. Larry was bleeding out. His blood pressure dropped and he became semiconscious and incoherent.

A second ambulance, driven by Edward Tudor, was called to the scene to take Larry to the emergency room of New York Hospital. Tudor realized the man he was putting into his bus was the same one he had passed hours earlier.

The well-dressed, out-of-place man with the attaché case was nowhere to be seen.

Chapter 13

HE'S GONNA SHOOT

THE three detectives from the Major Case Squad who had predicted that Zodiac would strike again early Thursday, June 21, were on the spot.

"He's got a window and he's gonna shoot," one of the detectives, Al Sheppard, had told Chief of Detectives Joseph Borrelli. Midnight was only a few hours away, and Sheppard, his partner Jim Tedaldi, and Larry Milanesi were no longer certain they wanted the honor of being the ones to call the Zodiac's next shot.

What if they were wrong?

They had been consulted because, in addition to their Major Case Squad duties investigating murders, kidnappings, and bank robberies, they manned "the Devil Desk," and were experts in occult crimes and cult activities. Some of their colleagues had dubbed them "the Swami Squad" and they were getting major ribbing.

The jovial Sheppard, with sandy hair and mustache, took the kidding in stride, but was worried. As an Emergency Services cop, he had won a chestful of medals for a wide range of heroic actions, from shoot-outs to dangerous rescues.

A former U.S. Army paratrooper who saw action in Vietnam, Sheppard had killed a bad guy in a shoot-out and had rescued dozens of people from bridges, building ledges, the East River—even a locked safe. The six-year-old son of a diplomat had accidentally locked himself inside the consulate's room-sized safe and was running out of air. Sheppard was the man who came up with the plan, which he and other cops put into effect. They smashed and chiseled their way through a surrounding cinderblock wall and cut a hole into the side of the safe big enough to pull the boy out. After Sheppard left Emergency Services and became a detective, he continued to attack problem cases the same way he attacked the locked safe—thinking first and then working flat out until he got results.

He and Tedaldi hit it off because they both went at the job at high speed. Tedaldi, a first-grade detective, was a summa cum laude college grad and a sergeant in the Air Force reserves. Tedaldi, whose black hair was beginning to streak with gray, spoke intensely, in rapid fire, usually sporting a wry smile. They were the kind of partners who were so completely in synch that they no longer had to finish each other's sentences.

They joined dozens of detectives, including Ray Liebold and Bill Clark at the 102nd Precinct in Richmond Hill, Queens, to trap Zodiac. The One-Oh-Two was just off Jamaica Avenue, more than thirty blocks east of Joe Proce's home. When the Swami Squad walked into the crowd of investigators in the detective squadroom, any hope they had of keeping a low profile vanished. They were already the laughingstock of some detectives, who asked whether they had brought along their crystal ball. But other detectives, like Liebold, had also noticed the twenty-one-day cycle, and were not scoffing. The Swami Squad took the jokes with a smile and were assigned to watch one of the dozen early suspects that had been identified in the East New York section.

Sheppard and Tedaldi had already contacted the San Francisco Police and sent them copies of the New York Zodiac letters, which California experts said had been written by a different hand. The Bay Area detectives still had

Zodiac suspects, and detective teams on the West Coast were also sitting outside those suspects' homes that same night, as they would during every subsequent "Operation Watchdog"—just in case one of them got on a plane to New York.

One New York suspect was a strange man in the neighborhood, who frequented the diner mentioned in the 1989 Zodiac letter to the Seven-Five Precinct. He muttered to himself and acted strangely. He also drew violent and obscene cartoons with odd symbols and tried to leave his artwork as a tip for a waitress.

The stakeout assignment was simple, to monitor the home of a suspect. If there was a shooting and the subject came home afterwards, he might be the Zodiac. If Zodiac struck and the man under suspicion never left home, he was eliminated. For the first hour or two, it wasn't bad. The detectives were used to stakeouts and they still thought they might get lucky, but as the night wore on with no movement from the suspects, doubt began to creep in with the damp air, especially after 3:00 A.M. The previous three shootings had all been between 1:45 A.M. and 3:00 A.M.

Meanwhile, on the streets of East New York, the underground economy had come to a sudden halt. The police presence drove the drug dealers off the corners. Hookers couldn't take care of business because they were being questioned about Zodiac. Uniformed cops and plainclothes detectives stopped, frisked, and questioned anyone who at all resembled the vague description given by Joe Proce and other witnesses of a black assailant. Between fifty and one hundred men were rousted that night, without results.

Detective Sergeant Mike Ciravolo rode around with a police electronic- and video-surveillance vehicle which recorded the faces of the men who were questioned. The first "Operation Watchdog" produced a lot of barking in the neighborhood, but the police didn't get a bite out of Zodiac. It began to look like Zodiac had stayed home, or the watchdogs had scared him off.

By dawn, most of the discouraged detectives had been sent home. Tedaldi and Sheppard, whose suspect—like all the other suspects—never left home, were feeling low. Reluctant to leave, they sat around the One-Oh-Two, listening to the police radios, hoping something would break.

Ciravolo was upset that the huge effort had not bagged Zodiac. Sitting at a desk in the detective squadroom, he poured himself a cup of coffee, put his feet up, and, with a sigh, began approving and signing overtime sheets for thirty detectives. Before he could finish, the phone rang.

"Sergeant Ciravolo?"

"Yeah." It was a cop calling from the Central Park Precinct.

"Sarge, the Zodiac shot a guy in Central Park."

Ciravolo's jaw dropped, his mouth wide open in amazement. *No*, thought Ciravolo, *he wasn't supposed to do that.* He dropped the paperwork and began asking questions.

"How do you know? Do you have a note?"

"Yeah, he left a note, with that circle thing."

Ciravolo got the bare details of the Parham shooting, hung up, and dialed Chief of Queens Detectives John Menkin, who had just gotten home.

"Chief, you're not gonna fucking believe this—he shot somebody in Central Park."

The news that Zodiac had struck in Manhattan spread quickly.

When Tedaldi and Sheppard heard the news, they got the Rush. They ran out of the precinct and into their unmarked car. Sheppard, who had taken a course in high-speed driving skills, flipped on the lights and siren and stepped on the accelerator. He felt vindicated by the shooting, but he wasn't happy. Someone had been shot and might be dead. He drove like a man possessed, like a Hollywood stuntman, through every red light in Brooklyn and Queens.

"I knew it! I knew he was going to shoot tonight,"

Sheppard repeated, as he rocketed toward Manhattan. He hoped the guy was alive.

"Can you believe this?" asked Tedaldi, who felt the same mixed emotions. They screeched to a halt on the Queensboro Bridge. Early-morning traffic was backed up and lanes had been closed off with orange traffic cones. Tedaldi jumped out of the car and tossed the cones aside. They were in Central Park, looking at Larry Parham's bloody bench, far sooner than Tedaldi thought possible.

A police bloodhound named Sherlock tracked Zodiac's apparent scent from the scene, sniffing the ground and pulling his handler west across the park and through Strawberry Fields, the tear-shaped section of the park dedicated to murdered Beatle John Lennon. The scent-hound followed the trail out of the park and down into the IND subway at West 72nd Street and Central Park West. The trail continued through the subway to West 96th Street and Central Park West, where it exited the subway and ended at a crosstown bus stop, where Sherlock lost Zodiac's scent.

The spent slug was cut out of the bench. Now they had two smooth bullets from Zodiac's occult gun. A search of the park and a canvass for witnesses produced almost nothing. Paramedic Edward Tudor told detectives about the well-dressed man with the attaché case, but he had seen him hours before the shooting, and his description was very different from other Zodiac witnesses.

Parham had undergone emergency surgery and was in critical condition but would survive. He was later interviewed in his hospital bed by detectives, including Bill Clark, who thought he was useless. Clark found Parham paranoid and incoherent. He had been asleep and did not see Zodiac. When asked if anyone had asked him what sign he was, he said yes, a round-faced black man with a mustache had asked him several days before the shooting. He was pressed for details, so a sketch of the man could be made, even though detectives had little confidence in Parham's memory or mental stability.

The note left on Larry Parham's bench featured the familiar Zodiac symbol and an astrological wheel. But this time, there were four slices of the circle filled in. Parham's cancer symbol had been added to the three previous victims. It also featured "The Twelve Sign will die when the Belts in the Heaven are seen," and the green "Zodiac" and "Faust" signatures. But the letter also held new puzzles.

Under the name Faust was a new symbol, an upside-down cross that had three sixes at the ends. The number 666 represented the devil or the Antichrist in occult circles. Above the new symbol, were two foreign phrases. The first was the French *Honi Soit qui mal y pense*, an expression translated as "Shame to he who thinks evil." Tedaldi and Sheppard immediately began researching the phrases and discovered the French saying had been connected with English knights for more than six hundred years, as the motto of the Order of the Garter. The Latin phrase, "Jacta Est Alea," meant "The die is cast," a phrase attributed to Julius Caesar when he crossed the Rubicon, a famous moment when he committed himself to either victory or death. Zodiac seemed to be saying that he was proud of what he was doing and intended to continue. He had crossed his own Rubicon—the East River—and there was no going back. He would let the chips, the dice, the bodies, fall where they may.

After a long, sleepless day of investigation, detectives gathered that night at a Manhattan precinct to look at the latest Zodiac note and plan their strategy. They had to start from scratch because the shooting had cleared virtually all of their suspects. The suspects' alibis were the detectives who had them under surveillance.

"Holy shit," said one investigator, looking at a copy of the note. "He's four-for-four. How did he know all their signs in advance?"

No one had an answer. Mario Orozco, Germán Monte-nedro, and Joe Proce had already told police that no one, including the gunman who shot them, had asked them their birthdates or astrological signs.

A couple of detectives who had mocked the Swami Squad in Queens just twenty-four hours earlier came over to shake their hands. Chief Borrelli began calling them "the Voodoo Team."

When Borrelli stood up to speak to his detectives that night, you could hear a pin drop. He announced he was setting up "a major task force" to catch Zodiac. The Zodiac Task Force headquarters, immediately dubbed "the War Room," would be located in an empty military build-ing at the Brooklyn Navy Yard.

"We've got another Son of Sam on our hands," Borrelli said.

Chapter 14

A STAR IS BORN

EDDIE'S scrapbook began to fill up quickly. The attention kept coming. Every day, there were stories on the front page of the *Post* in big, black letters: "ZODIAC STRIKES AGAIN," from which he clipped out all the stories about the latest shooting and how the bloodhounds lost the scent. The next day, the headline was "ZODIAC WRITES POST AGAIN," about the letter the *Post* got from Zodiac. There were also stories in the *Daily News*, even *The New York Times*, and on the television news every night. All about Zodiac. People in the neighborhood and around the whole city were talking about Zodiac.

The fear was spreading.

He read that the cops had formed a big task force to catch Zodiac, and that they found a letter that was sent to the Seven-Five Precinct the year before. Good.

But no one was dead. Eddie was angry every time he read about the old man, who was hanging on in the hospital. Why didn't he die? He was half dead already. It made Zodiac look bad. It made Zodiac's weapon look bad, like he was a bad craftsman. He didn't want people to think that. He opened his Moses magic book to page 160 and read one of the circled spells:

The frequent and earnest prayer of the 74th Psalm is said to defeat the persecution embittered by enemies, and will frustrate the oppressions of the self-mighty, wealth-seeking, hard-hearted people, and will at the same time bring them to a terrible end. The devout prayer of the 74th Psalm will effect the forgiveness of sins.

Eddie wanted forgiveness and he wanted to be in control of all things. He wanted the old man to die. He opened his white Bible to the Psalms, found the correct one, and began to pray, in a devout and earnest voice.

Chapter 15

ME IN THE PARK

THE day after Larry Parham was shot, I was working the phones at the *Post* when Zodiac's second letter to the paper arrived.

Half a dozen *Post* staffers had already handled the letter before I folded a clean sheet of paper in half, took the letter, and made several duplicates on the office copier.

"Why are you holding it like that?" a copyboy asked.

"Because I don't like ink on my hands," I replied, acting a lot cooler than I felt.

All of the *Post* employees who had inadvertently touched the letter were later that day fingerprinted by Detectives Jim Tedaldi and Al Sheppard, who arrived with several other investigators from the Zodiac Task Force when told of the letter's arrival.

Once those fingerprints had been excluded, any prints that remained might belong to Zodiac.

The new letter had many of the same features as the bench note, which had been kept from the press, including two mysterious Latin and French phrases, the cross with three sixes, the Zodiac symbol, the green Zodiac signature, and the astrological wheel, with the Cancer sign in a new slice. The details on the latest shooting victim were relegated to the bottom of the letter: "Fourth Sign dead shoot in Central Park white man sleeping on bench with little black bag shoot in chest June 21, 1990 3:52 A.M.''

It was obvious from looking at the letter that Zodiac was enjoying his fame but was very anxious to prove one particular point. Half of the page was taken up with Zodiac's writing and a little drawing, all intended to convince everyone that he was the same Zodiac who had killed people in California years before:

> This is the Zodiac I have seen the Post and you say
> The note Sent to the Post not to any of
> The San Francisco Zodiac letters you are
> Wrong the hand writing look different it is
> One of the same Zodiac one Zodiac
> In San Francisco killed a man in the park with a
> gun and killed a women with a knife and killed
> a man in the taxi cab with a gun

Below the diatribe was a drawing of a chubby Zodiac in a square-topped executioner's mask, with his symbol emblazoned on his chest. To the left, Zodiac had written ''mask,'' with an arrow pointing to it. To the right he declared:

> Me in the park
> is this similar no
> One Zodiac

This was getting interesting. If the California Zodiac had come to New York, it was an incredible story. In fact, it was too good to be true. I thought the serial criminal was protesting too much. He wanted us to think he was a heavy-set, middle-aged white guy from San Francisco. You didn't have to be Sherlock Holmes to figure out that meant he was probably young, thin, not white, and lived in Brooklyn. Or did he actually believe that he was the California Zodiac reincarnated?

The incidents he described, especially the drawing of

Zodiac in his executioner's mask, were directly from the Graysmith *Zodiac* book. Graysmith, when I reached him by phone in California, was appalled that someone was apparently using his book as a blueprint for occult murder. The former political cartoonist for the *San Francisco Chronicle* said his illustration of the original Zodiac in a hood appeared only in his book.

"Oh, my God. I feel terrible," said Graysmith when I told him about the latest letter. "This is a copycat. It's not the same guy. I hope they catch him."

When Graysmith first heard about the new case, he made sure a Zodiac suspect there, who had never been charged, had not left for New York.

"When I heard about the shootings in New York, I checked up on him and he is still here," Graysmith said.

When the Zodiac Task Force detectives arrived and looked at the letter, they asked the *Post* to withhold part of the message. By having information not known to the general public, investigators could quickly eliminate copycats of the copycat. They might also trap the real Zodiac with his guilty knowledge of the complete message. The *Post* agreed, and withheld the Latin and French aphorisms. When the letter ran on the front page the next day, there was a blank spot where they had been. But any advantage to police gained from the *Post* cooperation was short-lived. A few days later, the competing *Daily News* published both phrases. The publicity over the Zodiac Killer brought the nuts out of the woodwork and I began getting bizarre phone calls and letters from people claiming to be the Zodiac or one of his pals. Most were obvious fakes. I turned one letter over to police from an anonymous person who wrote a love letter to Zodiac, signed "the Seven Sister," because she claimed to be part of Zodiac's plan and the handwriting was similar to the real letters. It was a copycat, the experts said.

One morning, a man called the city desk and asked for me. The copyboy who answered the phone ran over to my desk and told me "a guy who says he's Zodiac" was on the line.

"Kieran, this is the Zodiac speaking."

My stomach sank and my mind raced when I heard those words, but I knew it was probably a crank caller. I didn't think the Zodiac Killer was dumb enough to use the phone. But since his idol in California did make phone calls, he might do it.

"I have a message for you that I want you to print," he said, in a calm voice. I grabbed my tape recorder and plugged it into the phone.

"Okay, but how do I know you're who you say you are? Anybody can pick up the phone and say they're Zodiac."

"I know your sign."

"Okay, what's my sign?"

"You will save a life if you print my message," he said, making it obvious he meant mine.

"What's my sign?" I pressed. As soon as he hesitated, I knew he was a fake. The next day, he dropped a letter off at the front desk that referred to the phone call and asked me if I could sleep at night. It was signed "Orion." His life-or-death message turned out to be a ridiculous poem about two little girls fighting over curly hair and split ends. The handwriting was nothing like Zodiac's.

On June 29, after a week on the streets of East New York, speaking to cops, detectives, hookers, residents, store owners, gravediggers, and fortune tellers, I drove into Queens to cover Joe Proce's funeral. Joe had been recovering. He was transferred out of the intensive care unit and was about to be released from Jamaica Hospital when he mysteriously took ill and died on Sunday, June 24. Police immediately investigated the unexpected death, fearing foul play, but an autopsy showed Joe died of diffuse peritonitis, an infection of the abdominal cavity, apparently caused by the gunshot wound that perforated his kidney and intestines. The hospital staff had noticed nothing unusual before Joe died. Anyone with such a virulent infection should have run a raging fever, as the body fought back but, strangely, he never did. His vital signs and temperature had been normal until he became unconscious and slipped into a terminal coma. The doctors told the police that the only explanation for the unusual death was that Joe never developed a fever or other symptoms of the peritonitis because his body simply never fought back against the deadly attack. The only witness known to have spoken to Zodiac face-to-face was dead.

Only a handful of Joe's relatives gathered at his parish church, the redbrick St. Thomas the Apostle Roman Catholic Church not far from his home. The smell of burning incense was added to the scent of the fresh floral bouquets on the altar, as the mass began. From the pulpit, Father Joseph Wilson appealed directly to the Zodiac Killer to stop shooting people and get help.

"You are troubled and you should get help. Go to your clergyperson . . . playing with people's lives like this, and harming them, is not the way to happiness," Wilson said.

"Our city is going through a very difficult time in its history. Joseph has been caught up in one chapter of that tragedy. The killer is probably a twisted and tortured person himself. It is so senseless and purposeless. It's really a very sad situation."

The simple hymn "Be Not Afraid," sung by a lone female vocalist, echoed throughout the church.

After the service, Joe's metal casket, covered with an American flag, was taken out into the brilliant sunshine, placed in a black hearse, and driven out to the Calverton National Cemetery on Long Island. Joe was lowered into a grave marked with a simple white cross, next to his fellow veterans. Standing on the green grass of the graveyard, a uniformed military honor guard raised their seven rifles and fired three times into the air of the sunny, sunny day.

* * *

At the Brooklyn Navy Yard, two empty rooms in Building 27, the old Officer's Club, were transformed by police, literally overnight, into the headquarters of the Zodiac Task Force. Several desks and a blackboard were put into an empty glass-walled inner office, which became the inner sanctum for several bosses. The surrounding large, open room was filled with desks, tables, and file cabinets, which quickly began filling up. Telephones bearing the phone number published in the papers began ringing as soon as they were plugged in. It looked like a TV telethon in which the operators wore guns.

"Hello, Zodiac Task Force. Hello, Zodiac Task Force. Hello, Zodiac Task Force," the ten men and women officers repeated over and over again as they answered the phones and wrote down leads from callers.

Chief Borrelli was concerned that the biggest criminal investigation since the Son of Sam case not be compromised by leaks to the press. Borrelli, who began every press conference by reminding reporters that there were two *R*'s and two *L*'s in his last name, was not averse to publicity and wanted to use it to advantage, but he feared the press would get underfoot and interfere with the investigation of promising leads, as had happened in the Berkowitz case. He instituted strict security. He was the only one authorized to speak about the case to the press.

The Brooklyn-born Borrelli, fifty-eight, started out as a minor-league baseball player before he became a cop. As a captain, he was the number two man on the Son of Sam Task Force. When asked what both serial killer cases had in common, Borrelli placed his hand over his heart and said, "They both give me agita," using the Italian word for stressful heart palpitations. He encouraged detectives to use their own initiative, telling them, with a shrug, "If it's not illegal or immoral, and you think it might work, why not give it a try?" This approach would soon bring psychics into the investigation, as well as a few other unorthodox investigative techniques.

For the first time, a new computer scanning and cross-referencing system was used. Phone tips were assigned to detectives, who went out, investigated, and then returned and filed reports. The reports were scanned into the computer. Any cross-references of names or addresses or other common factors would pop up electronically, a red flag to investigators. The idea was to centralize and compartmentalize the massive amount of data that began to flood in as a direct result of the publication of the Zodiac likeness, which had been dubbed "The Evil Al Roker," after the funny WNBC-TV weatherman it vaguely resembled. In fact, two callers actually called the hot line and told police Al Roker himself was the crazed gunman. Since he did not fit the profile of the killer being developed, Roker was never a suspect and was not questioned.

As they checked out the flood of tips from the sketch, detectives also geared up for another "Operation Watchdog" night in East New York on July 12—the twenty-first day after the Parham shooting. Each such operation cost the city twenty-five thousand dollars in police overtime. It was a tough situation for detectives. They were supposed to prevent shootings, but they knew their best shot at Zodiac was to catch him in the act, shooting by starlight.

"Operation Watchdog is in effect," announced a police radio dispatcher over the air, at 10:00 P.M. on July 11. One disrespectful cop howled like a werewolf into his radio, and a night of Zodiac lunacy began.

Detectives who left to pursue leads quickly realized they were being followed by a parade of press vehicles. To thwart their pursuers, dummy motorcades of detective cars would speed out of the Navy Yard, lights flashing and sirens blaring. Once the media followed the bait, a single car would quietly slip out to investigate the real tip. Task Force detectives had been issued scrambled radios and used code names like "White Angel," "Blue Falcon," or "Red Falcon." Two police precincts, one in Brooklyn and the other in Queens, were designated as places to question suspects, in order to avoid reporters and photographers camped outside the Navy Yard. The Brooklyn precinct was code-named "Birdhouse," then, for some reason, "Cathouse." The Queens precinct was called "the Greenhouse." Undercover detectives, wearing guns and bulletproof vests under rumpled clothes, wandered the streets and tried to look helpless, as their heavily armed backup teams watched from the shadows. Unmarked cars filled with detectives cruised the streets of East New York, Cypress Hills, and Woodhaven, or sat outside the homes of new suspects. Other detectives cruised through Central Park and elsewhere throughout the city.

Zodiac caught the public's interest because anyone with the wrong astrological sign might be the next victim. Astrologers predicted the next in line to be shot would be a Leo, prompting many Leos to stay inside for the evening. But some citizens caught Zodiac fever and went out. Police kept tripping over gangs of Guardian Angels and other vigilantes who thought they were going to nab Zodiac. One group of Zodiac watchers held a tailgate party, guzzling beer and monitoring the police radios, ready to race to the scene of a shooting. One civilian in Queens questioned a black man who slightly resembled the police sketch and whom he thought was suspicious. The vigilante flagged down cruising detectives and told them he had caught Zodiac.

"I got him! I got him!" the man exulted to his wife, who waited in their car, as the detectives questioned the surprised suspect. As the incident was broadcast over the air, the press converged on the scene. A group of Guardian Angels in red berets, feathers, and raccoon tails arrived. They were eager to take credit and told the press they had also been following the man, who was questioned and released.

Another man who looked like the police sketch was picked up at 1:00 A.M. and questioned for three hours before being released. As he was leaving the precinct, another set of detectives stopped him and wanted to start questioning him. He told them about the detectives inside, who had just let him go. He was then given a note on police stationery so he could make it through the Zodiac patrols: "I have been questioned by detectives. They have determined that I am NOT the Zodiac." The hapless man was stopped every few blocks and had to produce the note several times before he made it home.

Zodiac, it seemed, had chosen not to attend the party in his honor. At dawn, after a night full of nothing but false alarms, all detectives could do was laugh and go home for some sleep.

After the letdown, many detectives began complaining the sketch should never have been released because they were unsure if Parham was reliable, or if the man he described was Zodiac. The pressure from headquarters to put out a composite drawing in such a big case had overruled such concerns. The troops also soon began complaining that the new computer system kept them in the dark and that they did not know what other detectives were doing. Homicide detectives, not computers, solved homicides, they said. The fancy new computer system also failed to stop leaks. Veteran detectives were furious when they found out about major developments in their own investigation from the newspapers. It was no secret that virtually every one of the fifty detectives on the Zodiac Task Force wanted to be the one to grab "the Zodster," or "the Z-man," as he was sometimes called. Sometimes it seemed the task force war room was too small to contain all the large egos at the same time. Suspicions about who was leaking information to the press caused further rankling.

"Is nothing sacred in this case?" Chief John Menkin bellowed in fury to detectives one morning, after he saw yet another Task Force secret in the paper.

"Don't we have anything to keep in our vest?"

Menkin was using an old cop phrase for information

kept from the public, which detectives used to eliminate copycats and incriminate the real killer.

Not long after Menkin's outcry, police got something to keep in their vest—the FBI laboratory in Washington, D.C., had actually mapped Zodiac's DNA. FBI scientists made the reasonable assumption that the killer had licked the glued flaps of the three envelopes he mailed to the *Post*. They tested the paper and extracted DNA deposited there in Zodiac's saliva. The test results, those strange columns of dark smudges, represented a DNA profile of the Zodiac Killer. The "letter lick" DNA success was the biggest secret investigators had, and probably the only one that was not leaked to the media.

The Task Force had Zodiac's bullets, handwriting, fingerprints, and genetic code. Now all they had to do was catch him.

While some detectives were checking out phone tips, others were pursuing other avenues of investigation. A major part of the probe concerned whether Zodiac had access to a computer database of his own, in order to learn the dates of birth of his victims in advance. Statisticians had already told police that getting the twelve-to-one astrological sign guessing-game right—four times in a row—was virtually impossible. He had prior knowledge. Was he a city worker? Did he work for the welfare department? Was he a census worker, a clerk in a check-cashing store? The latent fingerprints lifted from the Zodiac letter sent to the *Post* and the one left in Central Park were compared to thousands of fingerprints every day. First, they were compared to criminal prints on file, without a match. Corpses were fingerprinted and checked to see if Zodiac had ended up on a slab in a city morgue. Police mug shots and mental hospitals were checked to see if Zodiac had been institutionalized. The fingerprints of every cop in the department were also quietly checked, in case Zodiac wore a uniform. Then the hunt expanded into other military and civilian fingerprint databases, eventually reaching more than a million print comparisons, without a "hit." A Zodiac zealot was created in the latent print section, Detective Ronnie Alongis, who imprinted the whorling lines of Zodiac's skin on his brain, as a result of comparing it by hand to countless suspect prints.

Other teams of detectives reinterviewed the first two victims and began looking for common threads that might tie the case together. One of those detectives, who had also been in Central Park on the misty morning that Larry Parham was shot, was a huge, barrel-chested Brooklyn homicide detective named Louie Savarese.

Louie, forty, had black hair that had partially vanished on top, and a distinctive handlebar mustache. He looked like a lawman from the Old West, or a biker—which he was. He rode a Harley-Davidson on the weekends and had named one of his three sons Wyatt—not after Wyatt Earp, but after a character in the 1960's biker movie *Easy Rider*.

Under his suit and thin Western tie, he was an illustrated man. "Big Louie," as his colleagues called him, was covered with tattoos that spread over his body like blue constellations across a pale sky. His chest, muscular arms, back, and legs bore the names of his wife, Mary Ann, and his children, Wyatt, Lyle, and Louie Jr., as well as other major events in his life.

Seven years earlier, a robbery suspect stopped running away from Louie and his partner, pulled a .38 revolver from his waistband, took a combat stance, and opened fire. The detectives dove for cover and were not hit. It took Louie and his partner seven months to track down the guy who had tried to kill them. When they brought him out of a Brooklyn building in handcuffs, Louie was stunned to hear neighborhood residents cheering and applauding. It seemed their suspect had robbed virtually everyone on the block, and there hadn't been a crap game in six months because of him.

Louie knew what it was like to look down the barrel of

a gun and he never gave up on a case. He took murder cases personally and regarded Zodiac's taunting challenge as a personal one.

Zodiac was already getting under his skin.

Chapter 16

HEAT

FOUR days after the Central Park mission, Eddie was very happy to see a picture of the old man in the hospital on the front page of the *Post*: "ZODIAC—NOW HE'S A KILLER, Third Victim Dies in Hospital."

Good. The magic was working.

But Eddie was not happy for long. Below that was another headline, "Cops Have Sketch of Shooter." He looked inside, but there was no picture of the police sketch. He stayed cool, because they still said Zodiac was a black guy with a mustache. Eddie clipped out all the stories about Zodiac, including interesting ones with astrologers who predicted Zodiac's next move, and psychologists who said he did it to get attention.

Eddie did not have to wait long to see the sketch. A drawing of a fat old black man with a mustache was on the front page of the Post the next day, next to a headline: "THIS IS THE ZODIAC." The story, just like those in the other papers and on television, said it was the face of Zodiac. It was funny. Eddie was very happy.

The magic was working.

The following day, as he was adding to his Zodiac scrapbook, Eddie was reading another funny *Post* story about Larry Parham, when he saw something that scared him. Cops said Parham was paranoid because he thought

his doctors and nurses wanted to kill him. They were un-
happy, because they thought Parham might make a bad
witness. But, near the end of the story, Eddie was startled
to read that "cops have two faint fingerprints to work
with . . ."

Fingerprints!

It said one fingerprint had been found on the letter Zodiac sent to the *Post* and another was found on the letter
left on the bench in Central Park. Of course. Zodiac had
held the letters by the edges with his naked fingers in the
park, as the Seven Sisters looked down. Orion and the
Seven Sisters were the only ones who could stop Zodiac.
Had he made any other mistakes while under their accus-
ing gaze?

Eddie felt feverish with fear, but a detective quoted in
the story said the cops doubted the fingerprints would lead
them to the killer. "Unless this guy has a [criminal] record,
and his prints are already on file, prints are only good for
comparison purposes," the detective said. Eddie was safe,
he had never been arrested or fingerprinted, but if he was
arrested, they would have him. They were never supposed
to get fingerprints.

It was getting too hot. The heat was on. It was time to
cool down. He would start with the barrel of the gun. Once
that pipe was gone, they could never prove any Zodiac
bullet came from that gun. Where should he get rid of it,
a garbage can, a vacant lot, the reservoir in Highland Park,
the ocean at Coney Island? What other steps should he
take? What about his scrapbook?

One thing was certain. He would be in control. He
would wait until the time was right for the next mission,
when things had cooled down. No matter how long it took.
He would wait for a sign.

It was time to pray.

Chapter 17

ZODIAC CITY

ZODIAC Task Force detectives heard about psychic Jane Doe* after she announced on a national televison talk show from Manhattan that she could track down the Zodiac Killer with her psychic powers. She claimed she came recommended by the FBI and her specialty was "psychometry." By touching objects from a crime scene, she went into a trance and purportedly got mental pictures of the victim and killer at the time of the murder. She became a psychic witness to the crime. It wasn't illegal and it wasn't immoral, so the detectives thought they'd give it a try.

Detective Sergeant Mike Ciravolo and other detectives went to her lavish suite at the Plaza Hotel overlooking Central Park, where the television show had lodged the out-of-town clairvoyant. Doe was attractive, courteous, and dignified. The cops told her they would appreciate her help, but only if she did not tell the press. She immediately agreed to go to a police precinct the next day to do her thing and remain mum. But, she reminded them, she must have some object from a crime scene to hold in her hand. She wanted to feel a Zodiac bullet that had been fired into a victim. She had to hold it in her hand. The detectives agreed.

The next day, a well-dressed Doe arrived at the precinct with a shopping bag. Inside was a huge magnum of champagne and several chilled glasses, all for her. Once inside an interview room with a one-way mirror set into the wall, she began drinking the bubbly, explaining that it helped put her into a trance. When she was sufficiently entranced, Doe asked for a bullet and it was put in her hand.

The detectives were startled when the soft-spoken Doe suddenly fell out of her chair and began thrashing around on the floor, moaning in agony and clutching at her chest. She made references to a bench and the park and had apparently become Larry Parham, after he was shot in Central Park. Several detectives exchanged glances but said nothing. Once she recovered from her ordeal, Doe came around long enough to consume the rest of the bottle and try to get inside the head of Zodiac. She was bombed.

She fondled the slug again and was off, eyes closed, head lolling. "Oh . . . I'm getting energy . . . I see a big penis . . ." At least one detective stifled a laugh, but another detective began interviewing Doe, as if she were the gunman, as if Zodiac were sitting in the suspect chair. She suddenly responded to the questions in a husky, rambling masculine voice: "I live near a divided highway . . . in a brick apartment building . . . I live with a young boy on River Street . . . coffee shop nearby . . . I shot a man near where I live and work in the city . . . I have a scar on my left arm . . . I made my gun . . . I don't stalk, I walk around . . ." When an exhausted Doe was done, she told detectives she hoped she had helped them and they said they hoped so, too. Yes, they told Doe, there was a River Street in Brooklyn, near the East River. It's on the map, near a divided highway. They thanked her, put her into a car, and took her back to the Plaza. What they didn't tell the tipsy telepathic was that the smooth lead slug she had held so tightly during her performance was not from the latest well-publicized shooting in Central Park, as she had apparently assumed, but from Queens.

She was Larry Parham when she should have been Joe Proce.

Dozens of psychics volunteered their services or called the hot line with hot tips from the spirit world. But, after the "big penis" episode, as some called it, and a similar but less dramatic encounter with another publicity-seeking psychic, who claimed he knew the name and address of the killer, Borrelli exorcised psychics from the Zodiac investigation forever.

The fact that Jane Doe had been consulted by the NYPD on the Zodiac case somehow found its way into the pages of the *Daily News*, which struck back at their rival, the *Post*, with an exclusive bedside interview with victim Larry Parham.

"It feels like my stomach is gonna bust open," said Parham, who expressed fears he would die or be killed.

"Somebody wanted me off this earth. For some reason, somebody marked me as a beast or a devil. I'm not a beast."

Larry was not a beast, but he was a Zodiac suspect as soon as detectives looked in his little notebook and saw his handwriting and mysterious, religious musings. The cross symbol with numbers at the four corners looked eerily similar to the Zodiac's new triple six cross. Was Parham Zodiac? Or was he "Orion"? Were he and Zodiac doing the shootings together? Was Parham shot before he could "stop Zodiac"? Was it a murder cult headed by the "Seven Sister"? Fortunately for Parham, fingerprints and other circumstances eliminated him as a suspect, and he began to relax with detectives in his new, unfamiliar role of star victim. After detectives made him take a bath, he ate better than he had in years, courtesy of investigators like Liebold and Clark, who one day drew the line and refused to buy Parham lobster for dinner.

Just after the Parham shooting, a panicked woman called the Task Force to say a man who looked just like the Zodiac sketch had, a few days before, asked her birthdate at the Columbus Circle subway station next to Central

Park. She brushed the guy off by giving him a phony birthday.

"Oh, so you're a Leo," said the man, with a happy face.

When she read about the fourth shooting and saw the stories that Leo might be next, she called police and asked for protection. She was terrified. Detectives alerted the press that the woman was not a Leo. The woman hoped Zodiac would read the stories and not shoot her. Detectives watched her home, just in case.

"She's a litle scared now, but we still don't think he is going after women," said one investigator.

Because of witness descriptions, the confidential police psychological profile of Zodiac said he was a black man, twenty-five to thirty-five years of age—despite the fact that the vast majority of serial killers are white. The killer, who had no more than an eleventh-grade education, lived or worked within walking distance of where Mario Orozco had been shot, the profile said. After the violent acts, Zodiac would need to return to a place of security and safety, where he lived alone, or with an older female relative. He might return to the scenes of his crimes to fantasize about his killings. Detectives wondered if Zodiac had been one of those who saw a low-budget 1970 movie called *The Zodiac Killer*, which included a graphic scene of a hooded Zodiac, costumed incorrectly in a cone-shaped Zodiac hood, killing a woman by stabbing her twenty-four times, until she died. It was available for rental in East New York.

Every day, leads were being followed on the gun, the bullets, and the notes.

Investigators were thankful that Zodiac was apparently using cheap ammo and a homemade zip gun, which may have saved several victims' lives. The cheap ammo was relatively weak. A homemade weapon was less accurate without rifling inside the barrel, which made a slug spin like a football fired by a quarterback. Gases escaping around a bullet lessened the power with which a round struck a victim. If Zodiac only had a one-shot weapon, it probably explained why the witnesses were also still alive. Cops checked out anyone arrested with a smooth-bore zip gun or antique weapon.

To get another slug for ballistic comparison purposes, detectives gave Germán Montenedro a few drinks before he agreed to go back to the hospital and have the lead removed from under his skin. The lump of lead proved to be barely usable. It was not as pristine as the bullet that had fallen out of Joe Proce's coat.

An expert linguist consulted by the Task Force studied the Zodiac messages and concluded that the killer was a Haitian man between thirty and forty years old, who spoke Creole, and probably French. A paper chase to determine the origin of the paper used for several of the notes led around the country and the world—from London, to Switzerland, to Canada, to the Caribbean. Old and out-of-production, the paper proved to be untraceable.

Thousands became potential suspects but were quickly eliminated by print comparisons or other means. Dozens of subjects began to "look good" and were targeted for further investigation.

Detective Sergeant George Rice was getting frustrated—not because there weren't any suspects, but because there sometimes seemed to be a zillion Zodiacs, like in the Hall of Mirrors fun house at Coney Island. Other detectives thought it was more like the roller coaster at Coney Island, riding the rush of excitement upward, as a suspect looked more and more like Zodiac—and then back down to earth, as he, too, was eliminated. Some subjects were frustrating because they couldn't be eliminated or arrested.

Rice was a serious investigator who believed that a homicide detective was the victim's last voice on earth. But even Rice was amused when some of his colleagues tried to get a break on one suspect by grabbing his garbage before the sanitation men got it. It wasn't illegal, it wasn't immoral, but it was smelly. They found out a lot more about the suspect's diet than they wanted to know, but they didn't get the break they wanted. Mike Ciravolo was once able to arrange that a good suspect be offered drink from a pristine glass of water. When the suspect finished his drink and left, Ciravolo grabbed it with gloved hands and rushed the glass to the lab. But Ciravolo did not pop a bottle of champagne that day—the prints did not belong to Zodiac. Under various pretexts, detectives would hand brand-new glossy photos to a man under suspicion, and then collect them after he had left his fingerprints all over them. It was a very successful technique, but Zodiac had not yet shared a "Kodak moment" with the cops.

Those checked out as possible Zodiacs ranged from ranting derelicts to working stiffs, to a banker in a three-piece suit. One hot suspect was himself a murder victim. The public expected a quick arrest of Zodiac, but the veteran detectives knew how hard it was going to be to find the psycho in the haystack.

George Gold* looked like Zodiac. He was into astrology and the occult and had crosses hanging upside-down on his wall. His printing looked like the lettering on the Zodiac notes. Detectives were sure he was Zodiac and set about gathering enough evidence to make an arrest. Even after a fingerprint check cleared him, many detectives refused to believe Gold was not the Zodiac Killer and continued to investigate him. Perhaps Gold had purposely written Zodiac notes on paper he knew had been handled by someone else, the detectives told fellow investigators, who urged them not to waste time on Gold.

Ten years before the Zodiac shootings began, Craig Edwards* wrote something in a high school friend's autograph book that made him a Zodiac suspect in 1990: "This is the Zodiac speaking. I love to Kill. Killing is my hobby. I thought 'The Exorcist' was the funniest movie I ever saw." He signed the entry "Zodiac." The words were directly from the book about the California case. Edwards, a working man, was questioned and placed under surveillance. His school records were subpoenaed. He cooperated,

The third Zodiac message—sent to the *New York Post*—announcing the first three victims. (Courtesy of the *New York Post*)

This is the Zodiac I have Seen the Post and you say
the note Sent to the Post not Similar to any of
the San Francisco Zodiac letters your are
wrong the hand Writing look different it is
one of the Same Zodiac one Zodiac

In San Francisco killed a man in the park with a
gun and killed a women with a knife and killed
a man in the taxi Cab with a gun

mask → me in the park
is this Similar no
one Zodiac

Honi Soit qui mal y pense
Jacta est alea

Faust
6 + 6
6

Fouth Sign dead shoot in Central Park
white man Sleeping on bench with little
black bag shoot in chest

June 21 190

Zodiac

Zodiac's fifth message—
sent to the *New York Post*—
on June 21, 1990, including
the "me in the park" drawing of Zodiac in an executioner's mask. (Courtesy of
the *New York Post*)

A 1990 Zodiac Killer
wanted poster with the
original composite drawing
of a man who had asked
the astrological sign of the
fourth victim before he
was shot in Central Park.

WANTED
FOR QUESTIONING
"ZODIAC SHOOTINGS"

ABOVE IS A SKETCH OF AN INDIVIDUAL WHO PRIOR TO THE SHOOTING OF
A VICTIM IN CENTRAL PARK ON JUNE 21, 1990 AT APPROXIMATELY 0500HRS
APPROACHED THE VICTIM AND DURING A BRIEF CONVERSATION INQUIRED AS
TO THE VICTIM'S BIRTH DATE.

DESCRIPTION: MALE BLACK, 30-35 YEARS OLD, HEIGHT 6 FEET (APPROX.),
180-185 LBS, DARK COMPLEXION, BLACK AFRO STYLE HAIR,
SLIGHTLY RECEDING OR SLIGHT BALD SPOT IN FRONT,
MUSTACHE, THREE DAY GROWTH OF BEARD. AT THE TIME OF
THIS MEETING THIS INDIVIDUAL WAS WEARING A BLACK
NYLON SHORT SLEEVE SHIRT, "LEE" PRE-WASHED JEANS AND
SNEAKERS.

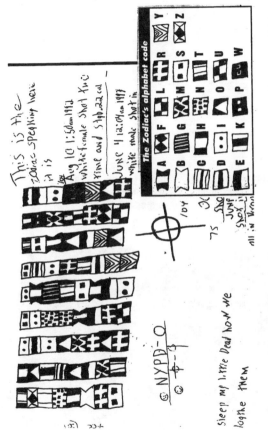

The sixth message from the Zodiac Killer—sent to the *New York Post* in August 1994, including the mysterious secret code symbols, a box score of victims, and the eerie phrase "Sleep my little dead, how we loathe them." Inset: The key to the Zodiac's code. (Courtesy of the *New York Post*)

Evil eyes—the 1994 composite sketch done by the *New York Post* of the Zodiac Killer, according to the recollection of the eighth victim. The likeness is much closer to the accused Zodiac killer than the original, publicized police sketch. (Courtesy of the *New York Post*)

Detective Joey Herbert (left, in front of armored vehicle) dons bullet-proof vest and helmet in preparation for hostage negotiations with Eddie Seda at 2730 Pitkin Avenue on June 18, 1996. Cop with bullet-proof shield (right) keeps his gun trained on Seda's window. (Brad Barnett)

The face of the accused Zodiac Killer—Heriberto "Eddie" Seda in June 1996.

The walk—Eddie Seda, clutching his blue bible (center), is taken to central booking after his alleged confessions, by Det. Louie Savarese (left), Det. Sgt. Joey Herbert (rear) and Det. Tommy Maher (right). (Andy Uzzle, *New York Post*)

Clean-cut defendant Eddie Seda walks into a Brooklyn courtroom on July 2, 1996. (Luiz C. Ribeiro, *New York Post*)

As a child growing up in Brooklyn, the only stars above Eddie Seda's head were those on Old Glory. (*New York Post*)

Eddie Seda's half sister Gladys "Chachi" Reyes describes how she escaped from her brother after he shot her in the back with a home-made shotgun. (Kieran Crowley)

Carmen Gladys Alvarado parts the blue rose curtains in her son's
room after the police search. (Luiz C. Ribeiro)

told police it was just a gag, and was eliminated as a suspect.

Albert Samuels* was a strange college student with a criminal record, including weapons possession. His handwriting resembled the Zodiac notes and some associates thought he might be Zodiac. Also, his initials were repeated several times vertically in one of the Zodiac messages. His non-Zodiac fingerprints cleared him.

Ted Victor* a white, twenty-two-year-old stockbroker, was a victim of equal opportunity suspicion. He was questioned and fingerprinted as a Zodiac suspect because he took an occult book out of the public library. "It's like out of *The Twilight Zone* to have these two detectives show up and question you for an hour and a half," Victor told me, while he was still a suspect.

Vinnie Santini never knew he was a Zodiac Killer suspect, because he was already dead on the floor of his Brooklyn apartment when he fell under suspicion. Police found a strange satanic book in Santini's apartment. When they opened it, they found a cryptic note with dates and exact times that fell within Zodiac's nighttime shooting hours. An exhaustive investigation found no new murders or Zodiac-style shootings on those dates or times. Santini was in the clear.

Richard Thomas* was a black man in his mid-thirties who could have used the Zodiac sketch on his driver's license. The resemblance was striking. He lived with his wife and children in East New York, near the shooting scenes. He was known in the neighborhood as a very religious man who often quoted scripture to strangers. When he was walking home from work one night, police picked him up and questioned him for hours. The press was tipped off that a Zodiac suspect was being grilled and were waiting outside the Seven-Five Precinct by the time detectives determined Thomas was guiltless. They had to sneak him hurriedly out the back door of the precinct to avoid the cameras.

"Maybe," a nervous Thomas wondered aloud, "I should shave my mustache?"

One anonymous woman, who worked at a Long Island alarm company, called on June 26, to say one of her co-workers from Brooklyn looked just like the sketch and was acting and talking strangely. She was convinced he was insane and that he was the Zodiac Killer. Because the man was an immigrant, his fingerprints were on file with the federal government. They were later checked and the man was eliminated as a Zodiac suspect without ever being questioned by the NYPD. The man, who rode the Long Island Rail Road to and from his job, was named Colin Ferguson.

That same day, Mayor David Dinkins held a press conference to announce a ten-thousand-dollar reward for the capture of Zodiac. Dinkins, with his usual dignified understatement, called the killer "A twisted individual with a distorted notion of his role in life." A few weeks later, Dinkins received a letter from a twisted individual claiming to be Zodiac, who said he would stop killing if controversial civil rights activist Al Sharpton were arrested. It was obviously written by a different hand from the Zodiac letters, but that didn't mean the guy wasn't also armed and dangerous. Security around Dinkins was increased. The letter was one of numerous copycats, all of which had to be investigated and eliminated.

Police warned the public that telling a stranger your birthday could mean your life. Some women stopped wearing birthstone jewelry, to prevent a watchful Zodiac from marking them as his next victim. Women who once smiled and flirted with men who inquired about their signs, now called a cop. Wives reported their estranged husbands. People suddenly decided their unfriendly neighbor, landlord, or relative was the Zodiac Killer.

"People are going crazy over this," said one investigator, as the calls poured into the Zodiac Task Force hot line.

"I know who Zodiac is, he's my ex-husband," or neighbor, or landlord, or boss, the callers claimed, in hushed tones.

"I just saw Zodiac" in a Laundromat, at a newsstand, or on the street, they yelled breathlessly into the phone. Most were sincere but mistaken. Some were out for revenge. One caller reported a man who was a dead ringer for the sketch and carried a gun. The man carried a gun because he was a police lieutenant, who was not happy to see Task Force detectives at his door, asking him if he was the Zodiac Killer. Half the cabbies in New York called, convinced Zodiac had been in their back seat.

"People can explain away drug shootings, but the random killer who stalks the streets always strikes a great deal of terror," said Thomas Repetto of the Citizens' Crime Commission. "Everybody wants to know who is he going to strike next, and where."

"It could be the guy next door," said a college student in East New York. "Everybody's looking behind their back, making sure they're not number five."

The Swami Squad—Detectives Tedaldi, Sheppard, and Milanesi—continued their researches into the astrological and occult aspects of the case, as well as questioning and surveilling suspects. The Zodiac symbol, they found, might be a Celtic cross, an ancient sign of sexual union. Or it might be an astrological par of fortune symbol, representing the wheel of the seasons. Or, it could represent a Wotan cross, which also symbolized the joining of male and female.

Astronomer Gregory Matloff, Ph.D., told them what constellations had been in the sky at the times of the shootings. He told them the Parham shooting was just a few hours before the spring equinox. The sun was moving into the sign of Cancer, just as the man with the Cancer sign was shot. Matloff, a professor of astronomy at New York University and the New School for Social Research, was consulted repeatedly by the Zodiac Task Force, who went on alerts when the stars might be right for murder. Matloff believed Zodiac may have been practicing an ancient form of worship that predated current astrology. Zodiac, he said, might believe that Orion and the Seven Sisters were actual supernatural beings in the sky. In mythology, the vain Orion boasted no animal on earth could conquer him. He was stung by a scorpion and blinded. He was then told to walk east to regain his sight. He was thrown up into the sky, and Scorpio followed in pursuit. Orion himself pursued the Seven Sisters, who fled from him.

The Swami Squad did a lot of research in the main branch of the New York Public Library in Manhattan, the one flanked by the famous stone lions on Fifth Avenue. They examined the works of occult British author Aleister Crowley, whose book *The Law Is for All*, advocated weeding out the weak from society. Milanesi found a card left in the book with a pentagram, lightning, and occult star symbols written on it. They took the book and card to check for fingerprints and got subpoenas for library call cards for Crowley's book there and elsewhere, hoping that a previous occult researcher was Zodiac. Detective Sergeant George Rice found that a local library in East New York was missing its hardcover copy of the Graysmith *Zodiac* book. Did Zodiac steal it?

In July, a man claiming to be Zodiac issued a death threat by phone against former city Parks and Recreation Commissioner Henry Stern. The caller demanded five thousand in cash be left in an envelope on a bench in Central Park. Cops staked out the bench, but the extortionist never showed.

"Is that all I'm worth, five thousand dollars?" asked Stern, then the president of the Citizens' Group, when told of the threat by *Post* reporter Marsha Kranes.

That same week, a man claiming to be Zodiac called the Task Force and said he would strike again. The call was never verified, but it was taken seriously by detectives.

A subway trap to snare Zodiac was planned, and appeared on the front page of the *Post*. The plan to shut down the system to nab one man was unprecedented. But, since Zodiac read the *Post*, it would hardly have been a surprise to him.

In late July, Borrelli had detectives check parking tickets in the areas of the shootings, perhaps hoping to catch Zodiac the same way the Son of Sam had been tripped up.

When the next ''Operation Watchdog'' arrived on August 2, eleven Zodiac suspects were placed under surveillance. Cops picked up a man shooting a slingshot at cars on the Van Wyck Expressway. He briefly became a Zodiac candidate when it was discovered he was carrying how-to books on murder and astrology in a duffel bag. A few days later, a subway fare-beater, carrying identification for several aliases, was arrested carrying a subway map with Zodiac symbols and strange writing. The man claimed he found the map, and was another disappointment to detectives.

The last shot for ''Operation Watchdog'' came on August 23. Borrelli announced that if Zodiac stayed home, the Task Force would be reduced.

''Basically, everyone feels that tomorrow night is a key night,'' he said.

It turned out to be a silent night, not just for Zodiac. Death and Zodiac both took a holiday. There were no murders around the city between midnight and 5:00 A.M., which is very unusual during good weather in a city that averaged five murders a night. I rode around in a brand-new Cadillac with *Post* photographer Joe DeMaria at the wheel, who carried a motorized Nikon camera around his neck, and a .38 revolver around his ankle. I carried a pen and a notebook. We cruised around Zodiac's neighborhood, listened to the police radios, and rushed to the scene of any violence. We arrived at one scene before the cops, but were upset to find it was only a routine stabbing among friends. We waited until the cops arrived and then continued on Zodiac patrol until dawn.

The next day, the Task Force was scaled back and about half of the fifty detectives were sent back to other jobs. Borrelli was convinced that his Task Force had forced Zodiac to halt his killing spree, but he was disappointed that the huge effort did not result in an arrest.

When the Task Force disbanded, Tedaldi and Sheppard put in their papers and retired from the department.

Louie Savarese was no longer part of the Zodiac Task Force, but that didn't mean he was going to give up. He was his own task force and would never stop looking for Zodiac. He would never disband.

The open Zodiac case was given back to Liebold, who worked with Ciravolo and Clark and others back in Queens. They worked on it whenever time permitted and whenever new leads came up. There was no death penalty, but no statute of limitations existed for murder. The city and state of New York would always have a jail cell waiting for the Zodiac Killer.

"Okay, let's take the best suspects and do them again," said Ciravolo with a sigh, looking at a roomful of stacked cardboard file boxes, all bearing the circle-and-cross Zodiac symbol. "Maybe we missed something."

On a beautiful, sunny day in November 1990, the few remaining part-time Zodiac detectives went to the Hayden Planetarium on Central Park West in Manhattan, less than a mile across the park from Larry Parham's bench. They gathered there for an informal seminar, to hear a lecture on the constellations and future star positions relevant to the Zodiac case. A huge black apparatus in the center of the planetarium created the illusion of a night sky by projecting the stars—including Orion the Hunter and the Pleiades, the Seven Sisters—onto the dome overhead. Sitting in the dark, hemispherical planetarium, the lawmen looked up at the beautiful, artificial heaven above them, a zenith of perfect diamond stars set in a black velvet firmament. They took notes, as the stars accelerated over their heads and then stopped at certain possibly significant future nights and times.

The beams from the computerized equipment raced forward from hour to hour and night to night, like a time machine. The spinning stars and constellations flew across the sky.

Chapter 18

SLEEP MY LITTLE DEAD

FLOATING on Eddie's television screen, in blood-red letters, were the words of Edgar Allan Poe: "Sleep, those little slices of death, how I loathe them."

Eddie liked that. He carefully jotted the obscure quote down in his notebook, as the movie, a gory slasher flick titled *Nightmare on Elm Street III—Dream Warriors* began. Inspired by Poe, the master of horror, Eddie then created a phrase of his own and also wrote it down in his notebook: "Sleep my little dead, how we loathe them." He liked that even better, the sleeping souls of his sinners—waiting for him.

The New Line Cinema film, starring Robert Englund as the facially scarred Freddy Krueger, along with Patricia Arquette, Larry Fishburne, Craig Wasson, Dick Cavett, and Zsa Zsa Gabor, began with a nursery rhyme, the theme song of the villain of the film, Freddy Krueger. Several little blond girls were playing in a park or playground and skipping rope, while they sang about the claw-handed Kreuger. Freddy was a long-dead serial killer who used supernatural powers to stalk and slaughter his victims inside their nightmares. Freddy and Eddie sounded so much alike, it was like the little girls were singing about Eddie, as if the movie were about him. He paid close attention to the movie, looking for its message.

"One, two, Freddy's coming for you. Three, four, better lock your door," chanted the children on the screen. "Five, six, grab your crucifix, Seven, eight, stay up late. Nine, ten, Freddy's back again." Freddy wanted his victims to sleep because he could only kill them when they went to sleep. Zodiac had wanted the city to go back to sleep, so he could kill again, when the time was right. The city was asleep. The time was right. Eddie had that feeling again, that lust to kill. He knew he had to go out and look for victims. He had just been waiting for a sign.

Zodiac had gotten away with murder. Alone, he had beaten the entire New York City Police Department. Zodiac had become feared and famous—but his reward was to be forgotten. It was the one thing in his life at which he had been successful—and he could not tell anyone about it. It was not fair, but it was better than being in jail.

Or was it?

The windows of Eddie's room had bars on them and he spent most of his time there. He and his mother and sister, like many others, were imprisoned in East New York by poverty and locked themselves inside to hide from the nightmare of drugs and criminals and violence outside. Zodiac's secret was locked up inside him, but the proof was in plain sight. He had to be careful. If Eddie was ever arrested and fingerprinted, the cops would have him. He had Zodiac's fingerprints.

But being careful was boring. Eddie had just celebrated his twenty-fifth birthday. It was August 1992, two years after the Zodiac Task Force had their last "Operation Watchdog" in August 1990 before disbanding. It was too long ago. Zodiac had not had any attention in a long time. Without attention, he would be forgotten. Remembering the missions, even going back to the scenes where they happened, did not do anything anymore. It would have to be different this time. Stalking targets took too much time and was very risky. Taking the time to find out their signs and putting them into notes was even worse. He had put foreign phrases on the Central Park note, because he wasn't sure he could find out the Fourth Sign. He was lucky, but it was hard and it took almost nine hours. He couldn't do that again. He could not get caught, or even get arrested for something stupid. He would look for signs and go for targets of opportunity, like some of the serial killers in his books and the documentaries he watched. But if he just did hit-and-run and didn't know the signs of the targets, it wouldn't be the same as before. It wouldn't be the same Zodiac. What could he put in place of the signs? Something easy, something that would impress people and strike fear, like Zodiac. More phrases. What about a code, like the San Francisco Zodiac? He would have to work on that.

Eddie had learned that it was a blessing in disguise that the cops had not found the first gun and the note Zodiac had left next to his first target. The magic had protected him. It was much better for Zodiac to work by stealth and only announce his return when he was done, when he had completed all his missions and was back undercover.

He glanced at a stack of books on the table next to his bed, including several karate, martial arts, and espionage books, like *Hands of Death* and *Inside the Killer Elite*. Eddie was also reading a new book called *Legend of the Holy Lance*, a novel that was supposed to be true, about a meteor from space that was made into a magic lance and was used throughout history by Julius Caesar, Merlin, Napoleon, and Hitler, to name a few. Beneath that was an army camouflage manual and *Combat and Survival, what it takes to fight and win*, with a soldier on the cover, his face camouflaged by black and green paint. Books were one thing, action was another.

On the television, Freddy was cutting up a woman with his bladed fingers. Blood was spurting everywhere and he was very happy. The San Francisco Zodiac also liked to kill women, like the one that was lying down with the man near the lake. Zodiac killed her with a knife. He stabbed her over and over. Would the Fifth Sign be a woman target? A whore, another sinner?

He still had the guns and his other equipment. He had only thrown away the gun barrels he used for the first four signs. Without the pipes, they could never match a bullet from a target with one of his weapons. As he got ready for another mission, Eddie began to feel good. He consulted his star chart and took out his Moses magic book. It was time for the prayers and the spells, time for the anointing.

Time to see if the magic still worked.

Chapter 19

LUST TO KILL

WHEN Trish got the urge to roam, she just walked out of her apartment building on Hull Avenue in the Norwood section of the Bronx. She walked to Gun Hill Road and got on a subway. She liked to go places, meet guys, and hang out. Her doctor told her she had to walk to get oxygen into her lungs, to help her asthma. Of course, the more Marlboro 100's she chain-smoked, the less she could breathe, and the more she needed to walk.

It was a Sunday and the buxom, five-foot-one Trish was walking in her new powder-blue Nike sneakers. As she descended the steps to the subway, her brown shoulder-length hair, frosted with blond highlights, swayed gently from side to side. She wore no underwear in the steamy August heat, only black cotton pants and a black T-shirt with brightly colored flowers blooming on the front, like a garden at night. Unconfined by a bra, her large breasts also swayed as she walked. Trish liked showing off her ample figure. The mother of two children, Patricia Fonti had just turned thirty-nine. She was divorced and lived with a boyfriend, who, like Trish, was also a mental outpatient. They both took medication to control their schizophrenia. Her neighbors, who had genuine affection for her, could always tell when Trish went off her medication. One way they knew was when Trish put her makeup on heavy and garish and a bit crooked, like a clown. The other indication that Trish was off was even less subtle—she appeared in the summertime street, wearing only her black mink coat. She strutted up and down Hull Avenue like a model, flashing the fur coat open to anyone who passed, revealing her completely naked body.

"I'm beautiful," Trish would say. "Aren't I pretty?" as she proudly displayed her big breasts to anyone who passed. Her neighbors, Diane Costanzo and Joyce Pion, would run after her and try to convince her to get off the street before she got arrested.

"I'm hot," she replied, flapping the heavy fur coat. "I need the sun." Trish would laugh, as the women bundled her inside. Strangers mistook her for a hooker when she paraded around with her happy face and exposed herself, but she was not a hooker or a drug user and she had only one minor arrest. Trish had a lot of problems, but her neighbors liked her because she had a good heart. They bought her cigarettes, even though they knew they weren't good for her. They knew Trish loved summer, like a little girl, because it was the season when she was most healthy and was able to get around. All winter, every winter, she was bedridden with asthma and flu. Trish was physically and mentally depressed until spring. She sometimes did not go out for months, and often did not speak for days at a time.

It was a hot, foggy Sunday night and Trish was off on one of her adventures. She had hopped a subway in the upper Bronx and made one of her journeys, bumming butts almost from one end of the city to the other, when she ran out of smokes. She rode under the Harlem River into Manhattan and then under the East River into Brooklyn. Perhaps for no reason at all, she ended up in East New York, Brooklyn, near the YMCA on Jamaica Avenue, opposite Highland Park. Trish had finished her last cigarette. She had no idea that, above the clinging fog, the constellation Orion was rising into the sky, toward the Seven Sisters who were already in the sky. She did not know that her own constellation, Leo the Lion, was not in the sky. She did know she was out of money and wanted a cigarette and some company. She walked toward the park.

Highland Park was named for what it was, the highest land in the area—not, as some cops joked, because everyone in the park at night was high on something. A glacier from a prehistoric ice age had reached the spot thousands of years ago and left a huge pile of rocks and rubble behind, after a warming climate forced it to retreat northward. By day, the park was enjoyed by people who played on its ballfields and brought their children to the playground on Jamaica Avenue. By night, most families retreated inside their locked apartments and the park was inhabited by a different nocturnal crowd, those who were seeking different recreations. Some were homeless and were looking for a dry place to sleep, like the bridge overpass of the Interboro Parkway, which snaked through the park and the adjacent cemeteries. Some were there to party on drugs and alcohol, and some were there for sex. Others were there for religion, like the devotees of the Caribbean cult of Santeria, who drank blood in ritual sacrifices and left bloody chicken carcasses behind. In short, it was a normal night in an average public park in New York City.

Trish asked several people for cigarettes, but she didn't get any. She saw a guy in a baseball cap staring at her from inside the park. He was also dressed in black and was sitting alone in the empty baseball bleachers. He got up and walked toward her, saying something. She walked toward him. When she got close, she saw he was young and handsome.

"Hi, ya gotta cigarette?" said Trish to him, with a big smile.

"Yeah . . . I've got cigarettes," he replied, flashing a rolled up piece of paper that looked like a cigarette. "You want to take a walk?"

"Sure. My name's Trish." She followed her new friend,

who seemed shy. He led her to a set of wide, winding stone steps.

"How 'bout that cigarette?" Trish asked.

"Just follow me, and I will give you the cigarette," he answered politely, waving the fake butt and starting up the steps ahead of her. Did he think she was pretty? As they climbed, the bottom of the stairway vanished behind them in the fog. By the time they reached the top, Trish was out of breath. He told her it was just a short distance farther and led her across Vermont Place, into the borough of Queens, and up the grass enbankment of the Ridgewood Reservoir, which was surrounded by a thicket of bushes. The handsome guy stopped at an opening in the undergrowth and made a gentlemanly ladies-first gesture toward the dark hole in the foliage.

"Go ahead."

Trish walked ahead of him and ducked to enter the tunnel of branches. The light from a small flashlight appeared from behind her, pointed at the path, so she could see where she was going. It was not Trish's neighborhood. She may have suspected her friend with the cigarettes was guiding her with his little light toward a lovers' lane, but she didn't know the overgrown area around the reservoir was known as a lovers' lane for gay men. Suddenly, the small concentric circles of light vanished from the path and focused on Trish's back, like a bull's-eye. Before she could protest, something knocked her down.

Crack!

The .22-caliber bullet passed through her body and exited without striking any vital organs. Trish collapsed forward onto the ground, but was still moving.

Zodiac was startled. He quickly reached for a new bullet, reloaded, and fired.

Crack!

The target stood up again. This had never happened before. He reared back and delivered a karate kick that knocked the target down again, but she was still moving.

He pulled out his knife, but hesitated. Zodiac had never stabbed anyone before and he was afraid he would get blood all over himself. He was afraid of getting AIDS. The target continued moving and he knelt down and stabbed her in the back, and chest, and arms, over and over and over, like the California Zodiac, who stabbed the woman near the lake. She would not shut up or stay still, she kept whimpering and begging him not to hurt her. He kept stabbing her, the blade puncturing both of her lungs and a kidney, until he realized she had stopped moving and pleading, and lay facedown and motionless in the dirt. He stopped. She was quiet. How many times did he have to stab her? She had scared him badly. Zodiac had never struggled with a target before. He felt bad, because he should not have hesitated. Zodiac always took pride in being cold, in doing what it took to get the job done. He made sure he had everything and walked away. When he was far enough away, he looked at his watch. It was 1:50 A.M., August 10, 1992. He would write it down when he got home.

Was Trish dead when Zodiac left her, or did she regain consciousness? Weak from blood loss, she may have been able only to sit upright. Helpless, as her life leaked out of her and into the dirt from a hundred small wounds, Trish died alone in the dark.

Police in Queens were alerted to the presence of a body at the reservoir about eighteen hours later. A man had discovered the body and called cops. Trish was barefoot, her favorite blue sneakers tossed into the bushes nearby. She sat with her back against the black wrought-iron railing of the reservoir, her head on her right shoulder, her legs casually apart, right knee bent.

The first cops who arrived saw no signs of violence and assumed it was a routine drug overdose. But when Queens Detective Dennis Brooks arrived at the scene, along with detectives from the Crime Scene Unit, they realized it was a homicide. After crime scene photographs were taken, the investigators found that the victim's black clothing was soaked with quarts of blood. When they donned rubber surgical gloves and pulled up her shirt, they were surprised to find more than one hundred stab wounds. Clearly, she did not die from a drug overdose but had been the victim of a frenzied stabbing, probably the result of a robbery or personal dispute. She carried no identification, but the corpse would be fingerprinted, and if she had ever been arrested, they would find out who she was.

Detectives had more questions than answers. They believed her body had been in a different position when she was attacked. Why was a woman's body in a gay lovers' lane? Did she survive the attack and sit up herself, or did the killer, or someone else, move her after death? Perhaps a homeless person came upon her, tried on her small sneakers, and tossed them aside when they didn't fit. They searched the undergrowth, but they found no murder weapon, no witnesses, no suspects, and no message.

Chapter 20

HANDFUL OF BLOOD

JIM was broke. The unemployed construction worker had a little change in his pocket, but he needed another fifteen cents to buy a subway or bus token to get from Queens to his sister's house in Brooklyn. Jim Weber, forty, zipped up his New York Mets jacket against the light rain and fifty-five-degree chill. He could take care of himself and decided to walk through Highland Park.

It was just after midnight when he walked south on Cypress Avenue, with cemeteries on either side, toward the park. His blue jeans and sneakers were already damp. It was June 4, 1993, as Jim, a Libra, approached the site of the murder of Patricia Fonti, ten months earlier. The spot was just yards off his route, but Jim knew nothing of the death. Her routine murder received no press coverage. He turned onto Vermont Avenue, just a few hundred feet from the park, beyond the Interboro Parkway overpass. Was it the rain or the dark graveyards nearby that caused Jim to quicken his step?

Zodiac had been lying in wait behind a tree, just inside the park, near the reservoir. This time, there was no Orion, no Seven Sisters, just Leo in the sky. That may have been why things went badly last year, with the woman. He had staked out the area, because anyone who walked in either direction on Vermont Avenue, just north of the park, was confined between parallel rows of fences, like a trap. When he saw a lone target approaching, Zodiac bolted from hiding and rushed north on Vermont. He went through the fenceway, crossed the street, and came up behind the target.

Crack!

Jim cried out in excruciating pain as the .22-caliber slug entered his buttocks, just missed his spine, and lodged in his right thigh. He turned, and got a quick glimpse of a dark-haired man, whose hair was held back by multicolored rubber bands.

He was laughing loudly.

Jim, horrified, heard the man who had just shot him giggling with glee. It was a big joke. The man ducked into a hole in the graveyard fence, still laughing. He heard chuckling, even after the figure vanished behind the rows of marble headstones of Mount Judah Jewish cemetery.

Zodiac looked at his watch. It was 12:04 A.M. He hurried over the sleeping dead with a smile on his face.

Jim was only forty years old and he did not want to die. He struggled to his feet, felt his back, and got blood on his hand. He was afraid the guy would come back and shoot him again, so he staggered through the park, down the stone steps, and toward Jamaica Avenue. When he reached what he thought would be safety, it was deserted. He leaned onto a car, looking around for help, afraid he would see the laughing guy instead, returning to finish him off. When he finally saw an approaching police car, he waved at them with the hand that was not covered with blood. To the two cops who pulled up, Weber looked like another stoned or drunk "intox" park person.

"I just got shot," Weber told them. The officers emerged from the patrol car, as Weber's legs gave out. Dizzy, he sat down hard on the hood of the car, clutching his back with one hand.

"Where?" asked one skeptical cop, looking at Weber's bloodless front.

"This ain't no prank," said Weber, pulling his hand away from the burning wound. He held out a dripping handful of dark, arterial blood to the cops, who immediately called for an ambulance.

"Does this look like I'm joking?"

Chapter 21

HEAD SHOT

JOSEPH looked and smelled like the unfortunate soul that he was. He was a street person, and his blue jeans were dark with dirt and his once-white T-shirt was a filthy, grimy gray. Also dirty was his matted, shoulder-length brown hair, which was streaked with gray, and his shaggy, salt-and-pepper beard. Joseph Diacone, forty, was schizophrenic and had a history of substance abuse, but he was neither drunk nor on drugs. He was, however, wearing another man's labeled underwear, the result of a laundry mixup at the last mental hospital where he had received treatment.

The night wind had come up, blowing across Highland Park and cooling the July evening down to seventy degrees, by the time Joseph, a Libra, walked into Zodiac's fence trap. Orion and the Seven Sisters were not above the scudding clouds, nor was Leo. Zodiac was hiding in the dark bushes by the stone stairs when Joseph ambled past. He hated street people. They were evil. Zodiac stalked the target up the stairs, north on Vermont Avenue, past the reservoir on the right and the parking lot on the left. There was no one else around. When the target walked under the Interboro overpass and was in between the parallel fences, he was trapped. Zodiac got ready. The target he shot on the opposite side of the street the previous month got up and limped away. The woman last year got up and fought him. It was time to go for a head shot, to kill his victim. He moved up swiftly behind the target, who may have heard something, and began to turn to the right at the last second. Zodiac aimed directly for the head and fired.

Bang!

The snapping action of the zip gun's rubber bands had thrown off Zodiac's aim, causing the shot to travel downward and miss the head. The .38-caliber shot struck the five-foot-seven-inch Joseph in the right side of the throat, severing his carotid artery and puncturing his windpipe, before exiting the left side of the neck.

Joseph clutched his neck. He tried to yell, but gagged and choked, as blood and air mixed in his throat and his artery pumped warm blood out onto the sidewalk. He tried to stop the flow with his hands, but it pulsed through his fingers. He fell over and sprawled onto his right side. Bright red fluid poured out of him, swirling onto the pavement in a spreading scarlet pool, and then it stopped.

Zodiac ran away. He later stopped to look at his watch. It was 11:35 P.M., July 20, 1993.

Joseph's body was not discovered for hours. It was not removed until well after dawn, after Crime Scene detectives had done their work and taken the last pictures of Joseph Diacone. Investigators did not know his name. Joseph carried no identification, leading cops to suspect robbery may have been the motive for his murder. Detectives believed Joseph's name was the one on the label in his underpants—until they found that man alive, but not well, at Creedmoor State Psychiatric Hospital in Queens.

Until he was taken away, Joseph's sightless eyes stared across the street at the lines of gravestones of the Mount Judah Cemetery, which stretched into the distance. The skyline of Manhattan was visible just beyond the marble and granite slabs.

Chapter 22

EVIL EYES

DIANE liked to hang out in Highland Park, but she was neither homeless nor a mental patient. Diane Ballard, forty, lived about fifteen blocks away from the park, just around the corner from where Germán Montenedro was shot. She had heard about the Zodiac Killer, but the shootings had stopped three years earlier. Besides, Diane was a Taurus, and Zodiac had already killed a Taurus.

It was a Friday night and Diane was enjoying the breezy, cloudy October night in the park, even though it was chilly and barely above fifty degrees. She sat on a bench just inside the park near Jamaica Avenue, next to the playground where she had brought her children when they were young. Just after 1:00 A.M., she thought it was time to go home, and stood up to leave.

Out of the corner of her eye, Diane noticed movement. A shadow darted from the bushes to her right and rushed toward her. She turned, and saw an attractive, Hispanic guy with a mustache, black hat, gold shirt, and black pants, running right at her. He reached into his jacket and pulled out a big gun.

Diane looked into his eyes and saw evil. He pointed the gun directly at her face and she started to turn away.

Crack!

A ball of fire exploded in Diane's face.

Once again, Zodiac's weapon jerked downward as it fired. The .22-caliber round struck Diane in the side of the neck. The soft lead slug splintered in two, shattering nerves but missing the major arteries, before lodging dangerously against her spine. A flash of pain jolted Diane's body as she fell. She was disoriented by the shock of nerve damage. From the waist down, it felt like her legs were up in the air, but she could see them lying straight beneath her, on the park sidewalk. By the grace of God, the bullet missed her head, but she was bleeding profusely from the neck wound. She was terrified she might die, or that she might be paralyzed.

Those eyes, she thought, *I'll never forget those evil eyes*.

Zodiac ran swiftly out of the park. After he was a safe distance away, he took off his hat and looked at his digital watch. It was 1:13 A.M., October 2, 1993. Orion and the Seven Sisters were up in the sky and Leo was not, just like with the woman target last year. But nothing had gone wrong this time. The target saw his face, but it did not matter, because he shot her in the head. She went down and stayed down.

During the first stage, Zodiac went out on Wednesday nights and only struck his targets early on Thursdays. He shot the first three targets only when Leo was in the sky and Orion and the Seven Sisters were not. The Fourth Sign would have also been shot under that same magical arrangement of stars if he had not been delayed so many hours by the Zodiac dragnet in Brooklyn.

But in the second stage, Zodiac was stalking or shooting victims in an opposite pattern—on every night of the week but Wednesday. He was not shooting on Thursdays and he was attacking hours earlier in the evening. Like before, male targets were shot when Orion and the Seven Sisters were not in the sky and Leo was. But the new female targets were shot when Orion and the Seven Sisters were in the sky and Leo was not.

Despite the fact that something always seemed to go wrong when Orion or the Seven Sisters were in the sky to witness his dark deeds, Zodiac felt he was in control of all things.

Chapter 23

CALL ME EDDIE

EDDIE'S guns did not look anything like the beautiful, shiny, expensive firearms in his gun magazines. The glossy cover of the new March 1994 issue of *American Handgunner* had an eye-catching picture of an incredible gun, with a bright red headline underneath: "Wow! Check it out! Exotic turbo-charged Speed Demon Pistol!" Eddie could not afford real guns, especially custom firearms like that. He could barely afford the ammo. His operation literally ran on a shoestring, which he used on some of his guns. Inside the front cover, a shoulder holster ad, titled "Subject of Intense Inspection," showed two plainclothes cops on a stakeout, using a telephoto lens to spy on a suspect. Opposite that, on page three, another ad featured a young man, guided by an older man, firing a gun. "You and Dad at the Range, Just Like It Used to Be." Eddie read the articles inside on tiny pen guns and the one about what went wrong with the Black Talon bullet, the slug that opened into a jagged metal claw and ripped its way through the body of a target. Eddie wished he could have afforded Black Talons when they had been available. No one got up after being hit with a Black Talon. The article lamented the passing of the murderous bullet, which was no longer available to anyone with the money to buy it— like Colin Ferguson, who used it to kill six passengers and seriously wound nineteen others on a Long Island Rail Road train three months earlier, on December 7, 1993. The article called the public and media outcry over the Black Talon an "assassination" of a bullet, and compared it to the assassination of President John F. Kennedy. "TV helped us live JFK's death, but it caused Black Talon's."

It had stopped raining and was beginning to clear up but the fifty-degree night air was getting colder. It was a Thursday night, almost spring, and the zodiacal light was back. More people were out on the street and in Highland Park. Leo was in the sky, near the zenith. The Seven Sisters were high in the western sky, chased by Orion the Hunter. It was time for Zodiac to go hunting again, time for the Ninth Sign.

On the way out the door, Eddie glanced at the drunken hobo clown clock in the kitchen. It was 10:42 P.M., March 10, 1994. He went down the stairs and walked to the corner. He crossed Euclid Avenue and turned north, across Pitkin Avenue, toward Highland Park. Eddie pulled out his weapon, looked at it, and put it back in his jacket. He was startled to see two white guys suddenly appear in front of him. One of them asked him what he had inside his jacket. A car was at the curb with doors open and he heard radios.

Cops. They had him.

Plainclothes Street Crime Unit Officer Brian Fleming stopped the male Hispanic subject, who was five-foot-eight-inches tall, one hundred and fifty pounds, and had black hair, brown eyes, light skin, and a scraggly Amish-like beard.

"What's that?" Fleming asked, grabbing the metal object.

"It's a zip gun," Eddie replied.

Fleming relieved the young man of a double-bladed, 3½-inch dagger and the zip gun. It was a foot-long pipe, wrapped with tape and rubber bands. It was a weapon, which meant a felony gun-possession arrest, which cops called simply "a gun collar." Fleming asked his name and where he lived.

"Heriberto Seda. Call me Eddie," he said to Fleming, with a silky smile. "I live right across the street." In Spanish, Heriberto is the same as Herbert in English, and means the glory of war, or illustrious fighter. Seda is the Spanish word for silk. Could Eddie cover up the war going on inside him with a smooth layer of silk?

Later, at the Seven-Five Precinct, Fleming asked Eddie if the zip gun worked.

"Yes," Eddie replied with pride. "I made it for protection. I have it for safety. Be careful. It's loaded; it might fire." He helpfully told Fleming how to unload the weapon.

"You have to screw the barrel of the gun off," Eddie explained. Fleming unscrewed the pipe and found a live .22-caliber round inside.

"You're under arrest," Fleming told him. He handcuffed him and put him in the back seat of the car.

They've got me, Eddie thought, as he was driven to Central Booking. They did not know yet, but, as soon as they test the gun, they'll find out it was the same one that Zodiac used on at least two of the recent targets. When they test the knife, will they know Zodiac used it to stab the woman target by the reservoir? Should he tell Officer Fleming now? It would make him happy.

Something made Eddie wait.

Fleming was not psychic. He had no way of knowing the quiet, polite man he had just arrested, who had never been arrested before, was the Zodiac Killer.

After he was fingerprinted and put in a smelly cell with street people at Central Booking, Eddie knew it was all over. They had Zodiac's fingerprints and now they had his. How long would it take them? It didn't matter. He would be in jail for the rest of his life. Police would find his Zodiac scrapbook and notebooks and all the other guns in his room, he thought. What would his mother say? He was very upset. He began to pray out loud. He begged God to let him go. Hours went by and nothing happened. He kept praying to the Lord. If God would let him go, he would repent, he would do anything. He prayed himself to sleep.

The next morning, he was chained in a line with the other prisoners and driven in a van to the old Brooklyn Criminal Court building at 120 Schermerhorn Street. He was ushered into a wooden courtroom from the back and sat on a wooden bench, as prisoners' names were called for arraignment. A Legal Aid lawyer represented the men and pleaded not guilty on their behalf. At that initial stage of criminal justice, a defendant could not plead guilty, even if he wanted to. When Eddie's name was called, the court officers brought him forward, but nobody mentioned anything about Zodiac. He was just another prisoner, charged with possession of a weapon. How could that be? The judge set bail and Eddie was taken out of court. By lunchtime, he was munching a stale baloney and cheese sandwich in a cell at Riker's Island, New York's island jail complex in the East River, between LaGuardia Airport and the Bronx.

Was the magic still working, or did God hear his prayer? Maybe it was just taking the cops longer than he thought to check his fingerprints and the gun. The .22 was only used on second-stage targets and Zodiac had not yet announced his return. Maybe cops really had forgotten about Zodiac and did not know about the last four signs. Eddie was very nervous. Every day, he expected the Zodiac axe to fall, but it did not.

He assumed that his gun had been sent to the police ballistics lab. He did not know that it was incorrectly labeled inoperable and possibly dangerous to fire. It was deadly, but it looked like a piece of garbage. Because the weapon was never test-fired, there was no slug available for ballistics comparison. As a result, when he was taken back to court a week later, the public defender got the charges against Eddie dropped, and the court records were ordered sealed by the judge. The lawyer explained that the card with Eddie's fingerprints on it would be destroyed, as if the arrest had never happened. It was a routine outcome on a minor case, but the taciturn defendant, when told he could walk out of the courtroom and go home, seemed amazed.

Eddie took the subway back to Pitkin Avenue. He had decided to dump his Zodiac scrapbook and notebooks and a few other incriminating items as soon as possible. His arrest had created problems at home. His mother felt religion was the answer and Eddie agreed. A day or so later, he went to the bookstore and bought his own Bible, a blue King James version. But was it his appeal to God or his original bargain with the devil that got him off? He promised God he would repent, but the Moses magic book said he was compelled to keep his deal with the devil. He would have to study and pray.

About a week later, Eddie saw Officer Fleming at the White Castle on Atlantic Avenue, and went over to say hello. He told Fleming about the dismissal of the charges and the sealing of his records. Fleming, like most cops, was not surprised when the system freed someone they had put behind bars.

"Eddie, you know that thing didn't work," Fleming told Eddie, referring to the zip gun Fleming had confiscated.

"Of course it works," an indignant Eddie shot back. "I test-fired it in my house. I covered it with a pillow and a blanket and test-fired it into my wall."

Eddie asked Fleming what kind of weapon he carried and what kind of load he had in his ammo. Fleming asked Eddie where he got his bullets.

"I got my ammo through the mail," Eddie replied. He told the cop he learned about making guns from reading about it.

"I read a lot," Eddie said. He said he also liked to read

such magazines as *Soldier of Fortune* and *Guns and Ammo*.

Fleming asked how Eddie made a living.

"I don't work. I live with my mother. We go to church together on Sunday. I get money by plugging up pay phones and taking the money out later."

Despite his admission of crimes, Eddie seemed anxious to convince Fleming he was on the side of the angels, of law and order. He said he hated drug dealers, and users, and the others who hung out on the streets of East New York and kept Fleming busy.

"I don't do drugs," said Eddie. "I hate those street people."

Chapter 24

ZODIAC IS BACK

IN Eddie's Moses magic book, it said every man had a guardian angel and an evil spirit, which controlled the desires of the flesh and awakened the lusts of the heart. Between the angel and the devil, there was a constant battle for supremacy. If the evil angel triumphed, then the man became his servant. If the good angel won, he would cleanse the soul and save the man from destruction. "The angel and his impulses come from the stars," the book said.

It was a Saturday night, and the devil had won. Three months after Eddie's release from jail, it seemed as if the magic was still working, far better than he ever imagined it could. It was a sign that he should continue. He had to keep on going, until the end. He was compelled to keep his bargain. He prayed and prepared himself and walked out into the cloudy, cool June night. Orion and the Seven Sisters were not in the sky above the clouds and Leo was.

Zodiac returned to the bushes by the reservoir in Highland Park. He was staking out the fence trap that had already snared him two targets. After a while, a meandering target appeared in the distance. A white male. The target was pushing a squeaky shopping cart. He wandered up and down Vermont Place and the parking lot, searching the ground and probing in garbage cans for deposit cans. From his spot in the bushes, Zodiac watched the target, who was oblivious to the fact that he was the subject of intense scrutiny. The target ambled toward the fence trap and was almost there when he turned around. Zodiac sprung from his hiding place and ran up behind the target. He drew his weapon and aimed for the head.

Crack!

Zodiac ran from the park and later, as usual, stopped to look at his watch. It was 11:09 P.M., June 11, 1994. Zodiac's Omega constellation, Leo the Lion, was just setting.

On Eddie's desk was a blue paperback novel, the 1993 bestseller by Jonathan Kellerman, *Devil's Waltz.* The cover of the psychological thriller that Eddie was reading featured a floating masquerade mask—black on one side, white on the other. In the book, a mother was suspected of causing her child's deadly illness.

The holy war between Eddie's angel and devil continued in his room through June and July, with much praying and chanting and cursing. On July 31, he celebrated his twenty-seventh birthday and decided to give himself a secret birthday present.

With gloves on, Eddie painstakingly copied his new, coded message, stacking flaglike symbols into nine vertical columns, creating a forest of mysterious totem poles. Just to the left of the totemic cryptogram, he jotted down an upside-down Taurus symbol, surrounded by a circle that was three-quarters complete. Below that, he drew a circle with horns on top and a cross underneath—the symbol for the planet Mercury, messenger of the Gods. Beneath the code, he made a box score. First, he drew a cute little frowning face and wrote "NYPD–0" Underneath that, he drew a line, then a happy, smiling face, followed by the Zodiac symbol and the number 9.

Cops 0, Zodiac 9. It was right out of the book on the California killer, except the Zodiac score was lower. Eddie listed the second-stage targets, with dates and times and locations and bullet calibers, and drew a Zodiac symbol nearby. At the bottom of the page, he wrote the phrase he had created in his notebook: "Sleep my little dead, how we loathe them."

The next day, August 1, Eddie mailed his new message to the *Post*: Zodiac is back.

Chapter 25

DECODING ZODIAC

WEDNESDAY, August 3, 1994, was a slow news day at the *New York Post*. Four years and two months after Zodiac's "Me in the Park" letter to the paper, copyboy Chris Plata found a strange letter in the afternoon mail. Bearing a "Love" stamp, it had been postmarked in Queens two days earlier. He gave it to City Desk Assistant Myron Rushetzky. *Post* Metropolitan Editor Stuart Marques was sitting at the City Desk, engaged in his daily search for "The Wood"—the front-page story. It was a dead summer day. He wondered what the hell he was going to put on Thursday's front page.

"You should look at this," Rushetzky said, dropping the letter on the City Desk. Marques looked at the page. There were vertical rows of small rectangles, filled with squares, dots, lines, and triangles. They looked like strange totem poles. To the right of the nonsensical symbols was scribbled "This is the Zodiac speaking here it is."

"Uh, oh," said Marques to himself, as his eyes raced over the page. Below the signature phrase of the Zodiac Killer was another list of shootings. Below the symbols was an unmistakable Zodiac symbol. He looked at the tiny sad face next to "NYPD–0" and the bizarre happy face next to the Zodiac symbol and the number 9. On the lower left of the page was scribbled "Sleep my little dead, how we loathe them."

Wow, thought Marques. He's back. But the letter didn't mention anything about astrology. It didn't give the signs of the victims, like Zodiac did before. Also, the writing was even sloppier than the previous Zodiac letter. Was it real, or a fake? Was it the guy from 1990 or was it another guy, a copycat? Marques picked up the phone and called *Post* Criminal Justice Editor Murray Weiss.

By the next day, Weiss had confirmed that the shootings were real and Marques had a Wood for Friday. Marques assigned several reporters to find the two new surviving victims. *Post* reporter Cathy Burke found victim Diane Ballard, and reporter Philip Messing tracked down Jim Weber. The *Post* turned the original letter and envelope over to the police, who knew about four of the five shootings. They had not been connected—until the Zodiac II letter arrived at the *Post*. Two victims were dead and two had been wounded. But cops never found the ninth victim, who may have been missed or only grazed by a bullet. No one knew whether the Zodiac Killer was back, or if it was another copycat. The *Post* front page the next day heralded the exclusive story: "ZODIAC II: Cops Fear Copycat Serial Murderer."

Four years after he had been shot in Central Park, victim Larry Parham was getting treatment for pain from his two chest wounds, and depression, caused by the Zodiac attack. Parham finally got his own apartment—a single-room-occupancy apartment in the Bronx, which he scrubbed and cleaned and kept spotless. He said he forgave the man who shot him, but he wanted Zodiac to stop shooting and give himself up.

"I'm tired of being stepped on," said Parham. "I have to go on with my life. I just hope they find him. I hope he don't shoot nobody else." Parham was not working, but was studying for his high school equivalency diploma.

Jim Weber said that his fateful decision a year earlier to

walk through the dark park "was the worst mistake I ever made." Weber had made a good physical recovery, but he was haunted by his brush with Zodiac. His blue eyes darting around in fear, Weber said the shooting had made him permanently paranoid and he trusted no one. When a car backfired, Weber jumped. In recurring nightmares, he found himself once again holding a handful of his own blood, once again under the gun of a laughing Zodiac— but this time, he was going to die. When awake, Weber could no longer hold down a job. He said it was because he did not want to establish a pattern. He never went anywhere near Highland Park. Now that Zodiac might be back, Weber made plans to move and go into hiding.

Diane Ballard's life was also ruined by Zodiac. She was able to walk again, but was troubled by recurring pain and neurological problems. What was worse, she said, was the constant fear.

"At first, I couldn't stay in the house by myself. I was paranoid," she said. "The way I look at it, it can't get any worse than this. I'm a walking corpse." The *Post* hired a former police sketch artist, who prepared a sketch of Zodiac II, with Ballard's help. The gunman she saw in the park that night was a Latino, with arched eyebrows, "vicious, evil eyes," and a mustache she said looked just like the one Hollywood actor Val Kilmer wore in the Western movie *Tombstone*. The sketch ran on the front page of Saturday's *Post*: "ZODIAC II: The Evil Eyes."

There was a sidebar story about the mysterious, flaglike symbols: "The Flags—Killer's Doodles Have Cops Baffled."

Saturday was my day off and I decided to spend it at my Long Island home, trying to figure out what the symbols meant. I was convinced they were some kind of code, because the California Zodiac had sent encrypted messages in symbols to the newspapers there. I looked at the nine columns, and realized there was one for each victim claimed, like some kind of satanic trophies or headstones. It had to be a code. I decided to take a crack at it. I had done research on cryptography and code-breaking while working on a historical novel about Edgar Allan Poe and had minor success. I had found a strange message hidden in a Poe poem for more than one hundred fifty years.

My wife, Riki, knew about my minor obsession with the Zodiac case, and smiled indulgently as she looked over my shoulder and saw me mapping out the weird symbols on a yellow legal pad.

"What are you doing?"

I told her.

"You're crazy." She laughed, leaving me alone.

I decided that each horizontal line probably divided one symbol from another. As I looked, I saw characters repeated again and again. It had to be a code. When I noticed that the last three totems on the right each had one less than the eight symbols of the other columns, I reasoned it was because Zodiac's coded message read from top to bottom and left to right. Maybe. I copied down each different symbol. When I was done, I counted twenty-three separate ones, almost enough for an alphabet. I was cautiously excited, because I thought it was the simplest type of code—one that used one symbol for one letter. I then did a frequency count, counting how many times each symbol appeared in the message. The ones that appeared the most might be vowels. I thought the one with two dark discs might be the letter *E*, but that didn't seem to work.

I knew I could spend days or weeks trying thousands of possible combinations of boxes for letters without finding the solution. I not only wanted to solve the code, but I wanted to do it quickly. I went to the only person I knew who had been a code-breaker—Riki's father, Al Nemser.

Al's wavy, black hair was threaded with gray, but he looked a full two decades younger than his eighty years. Al was a lawyer on Long Island and had a steel-trap mind. He had been a U.S. Army Signal Corps cryptographer in

World War II. He had also solved a code used by a Confederate spy that had stumped code-breakers since the Civil War.

As a child growing up in Brooklyn in the early 1920s, Al used to sled down the snowy slope of Highland Park's "Snake Hill," when the park was safe at night and the phrase "serial killer" had not yet been invented. In 1933, he courted his future wife, Tess, in the park—on the same benches near Jamaica Avenue, where, sixty years later, the Zodiac Killer shot Diane Ballard.

When I showed him what I had done, Al agreed that it looked like a simple mono-substitution cipher, but he said the sixty-nine-symbol message was not long enough to make letter frequency useful.

"We'll have to be lucky because the message is too short," he said in his distinctive baritone voice, as we sat down at his kitchen table. After various vowel combinations failed to unlock any words, Al suggested we try to solve the puzzle a different way—by educated guesses at its content. Since most sentences started with the word "the," Al tried those three letters first. It didn't work. Then I had a sudden flash of insight:

"It has to start with 'This is the Zodiac Speaking.' It has to," I said.

"Why?" asked Al.

"Because that's how the original California guy always started off his messages. This guy is a copycat. That's the way he would start this. He even used the phrase in this letter, in plain English."

"Oh," said Al. "You didn't tell me that." He wrote "T-h-i-s" over the first four symbols and they were all different.

"So far, so good." Al said, calmly. He then wrote "i-s t-h-e" over the next five symbols, it was immediately obvious the symbol with the two dark dots, and the symbol with the two dark squares, repeated to form the word "is."

"It seems to be right," Al said cautiously, as he filled in the rest of the letters.

"Yes!" I shouted, banging the table with my fist.

I got "the Rush" detectives had described to me. It felt great. There was also a "gotcha" feeling, a thrill of the hunt. The game was afoot.

We tried out different combinations of letters, and, within twenty minutes, had deciphered most of the message. But there were still some six holes in the decipherment:

```
THISISTHE
ZODIACSPE
?KINGIAMI
NCONTROLW
HOMASTER?
?EREAD?FO
RMORE?OUR
SHRUL?
```

Adding punctuation and using question marks where we were unsure, the message read: "This is the Zodiac spe?king. I am in control. Who master? ?e read? for more ?ours hrul?" Obviously, the fifth word was "speaking." Zodiac had apparently failed to shade in two areas inside the symbol for the first letter of the alphabet. We had to stop work on the code to get ready for a family birthday party that night.

After a night's sleep, I brought the code-breaking work with me to work the next day. I was the Sunday morning assignment editor and I had my hands full, deciding what stories to cover and which reporters should cover them. But the first thing I did was take another crack at Zodiac's code. Just like with a crossword puzzle, the answers I did not have the night before were suddenly obvious:

Obviously, the hourglass symbol was a *b*, obviously the chevron symbol was a *y*, obviously Zodiac made another mistake—he forgot to add two lines to the *t* symbol, incorrectly making it an *h*. The message I now had was:

"This is the Zodiac speaking. I am in control who mastery. Be ready for more. Yours truly."

I knew it had to be "Yours truly" because the California Zodiac used that phrase in one of his letters, which he had copied from a grisly letter written in blood by Jack the Ripper. "Who mastery" didn't make sense, but that's what Zodiac had written. After some more table banging, I called Al at home and ran my new letters and the final solution past him. He agreed and we congratulated each other.

Meanwhile, the phones were ringing and I continued to assign reporters who checked in. I called my boss, Stu Marques, at home and politely suggested he might have to come in early. I told him what Al and I had done, and that I wanted to write the story.

"I just assigned myself an exclusive Wood and a shrink sidebar," I told him.

"What does the message say?" he asked. I read it to him.

" 'Be ready for more'? " he repeated.

"Yup. 'Be ready for more.' and he signed it 'Yours truly,' just like Jack the Ripper did."

"I'm coming in," said Marques, and he hung up the phone.

The detectives I was able to reach on a Sunday either knew nothing about a solution or would not comment. I tried to reach government code-breakers at the National Security Agency in Washington, D.C., to confirm the solution, but they were so secretive they wouldn't even say the word "code" over the phone.

I compiled the list of stories and assignments for the day and turned it over to Marques when he arrived. He was familiar with my skills as a reporter, but not as a code-breaker. He was cautious and played the devil's advocate.

"But what if you're wrong?" he asked. He wanted official confirmation before we ran the story. I wrote the main story, about how Al and I decrypted the message. For my "shrink" sidebar, I spoke to a Bellevue Hospital forensic psychiatrist, Dr. Michael Welner, who said Zodiac II—based on the new message—was a sadistic, lonely "hunter" seeking attention. The killer wanted to "create intrigue with the codes. He wants to be glamorous, because he's a loser," said Welner. "It's very cowardly. His gun is causing a lot of people pain." Welner thought Zodiac might strike again, after the furor had died down.

By the time I had finished writing my stories, Murray Weiss had gotten confirmation from the cops. Police said they had consulted code experts, who had just reached the same solution as Al and I had. There was really only one possibility for the Wood:

"*Post* Breaks Zodiac Code: 'BE READY FOR MORE.' "

The next day, I discovered that Zodiac's alphabet was based on a maritime system of International Flags and Pennants, and got a copy of that chart. The symbols were doubled in the horizontal plane, in something called a "looking glass" alphabet code. It was likely created by placing a small mirror on the left side of each naval flag symbol. Two of the letters, *k* and *t*, had to be altered, because they would have looked the same in the mirror.

I told Stu Marques that we had to send a message to Zodiac in his own code in Tuesday's paper. I began working on a message based on information from the California Zodiac case. The idea was to intrigue the cautious killer and keep him writing to the *Post*. The police liked anything that would give them more information, and possibly enough evidence to catch Zodiac. But *Post* Editor Ken Chandler had a better idea. Chandler wanted the *Post* to trap the Zodiac Killer, or arrange for his surrender—by phone. The plan was to use the code to tell Zodiac to call us on a special phone line. But the killer had not used numbers in his code. There were number symbols in the maritime flag code, but they were triangles, not rectangles. The symbols would look very different. The idea was to do it in a low-key way. Instead, I encoded the words "Urgent, please call . . . " followed by the phone number—spelled out in words. I arranged the message in nine columns, just like Zodiac's original message, so it would look the same to the casual observer. We had already run the code key in the paper, making it a snap for anyone to decode the message. We expected our plan to be detected and publicized by the *Daily News*, but it wasn't. Virtually no one noticed that the Zodiac symbols we ran the next day were in a different order. I was grateful to several television stations, who actually ran our message to Zodiac on the screen, incorrectly identifying it as Zodiac's original code.

Would Zodiac notice our return message? Would the cautious serial killer feel enough in control to pick up a telephone and call us? He did not call on the day our message to him ran in the paper, or the next day, or the next week, which was not surprising. He may have feared a trap.

Meanwhile, Al and I were media celebrities. Al made several television appearances and I spoke on several radio shows. I accepted an invitation to tape an appearance on the nationally syndicated *Rolanda Watts* television show, hoping to get another message to Zodiac. I consulted Dr. Welner again, who advised me to tempt Zodiac with an appeal that he move "to the next phase." Also appearing with me were author Robert Graysmith and retired Detective Sergeant Mike Race, a former homicide detective in the 75th Precinct.

After I opened the segment with a description of the Zodiac case, I said that the Zodiac Killer "could be watching this show right now and, as a matter of fact, there's something I'd like to say to him. In his coded message he said—mimicking the San Francisco's Zodiac, the original—'I am in control.' I'd like him to prove it by sending another message, before he hurts anyone else, because I think it's time for this to move on to the next phase." During the next break in the taping, Mike Race turned to me:

"Buddy, that's some death wish you've got," he said.

"Whaddya mean?"

"You just challenged a serial killer to come after you."

"No I didn't, I just asked him to write to . . ."

"You said send a message. This guy knows people's birthdays before he shoots them. If he has access to a computer . . ."

"Oh. Right." Race didn't have to finish the thought. Zodiac might be able to find out what my sign was and where I lived. He might decide to send me a loud message I wasn't expecting. I quickly found out that paranoia is a contagious disease. When I got home, I showed Riki the sketch of Zodiac II and warned her to be careful. Six weeks after the show aired, I had not heard from Zodiac— but someone broke into our home while we were out to dinner, setting off the burglar alarm. The police found a back door wide open but nothing had been taken. A few weeks later, someone tried to force open the same door at 4:00 A.M., setting off the alarm again. I had to work very hard to convince myself that it was probably a coincidence. I knew that it was highly unlikely that the Zodiac Killer would leave his usual hunting grounds in Brooklyn and Queens and begin stalking the Long Island suburbs. I took further security precautions and the break-in attempts stopped.

Al and I had decoded his words, but that was just what Zodiac wanted us to do. We hadn't learned anything about him, other than the fact that he was a bad speller who liked to kill people, a happy warrior who sneaked over the graves of honored war dead to shoot unarmed people in the back. He and his identity were still an enigma. In Highland Park, Zodiac posters had been plastered over every pole and wall by Guardian Angels, who were roaming the neighborhood, day and night. With his deadly return, Zodiac had achieved cult status.

"Everybody knows he lives up in one of the cemeteries, inside one of the crypts," one resident told me. "He only comes out at night."

That particular rumor, and the use of the graveyards by Zodiac as an escape route in one of the new shootings, caused the newly formed Zodiac II Task Force to conduct a thorough search of the cemeteries. They did find a few homeless people who had set up housekeeping alongside the dead in tombs, but none of those ghouls turned out to be Zodiac.

Citizens, detectives, and reporters broke into three groups—it was the same guy, it wasn't the same guy, and I don't know. Retired Swami Squad detectives Al Sheppard and Jim Tedaldi thought Zodiac II was probably not Zodiac I. Detective Sergeant Mike Ciravolo, who had also recently retired, agreed. I was in all three groups, sometimes on the same day. I thought it might be the same guy trying to look different—but why? Could Zodiac II actually be a third Zodiac—a copycat of a copycat?

"Christ," joked one exasperated detective, "it's a fuckin' franchise."

Chapter 26

REPENTANCE

EDDIE walked up the brick steps in the August heat and into the redbrick Saint Fortunata's Roman Catholic Church on Crescent Street, near Linden Boulevard. Above the front doors of the house of worship was a bell tower, containing a single bell, topped by a large cross. As he entered the church, Eddie passed the statue of the prostrate namesake of the parish, Saint Fortunata, in the vestibule. Saint Fortunata was a virgin who renounced marriage and gave her life to God. A convert from Palestine, she was a Christian martyr put to death in Rome around A.D. 303 by the Roman Emperor Diocletian, during the last persecution of the Christians. Eddie was also a virgin who had renounced marriage and given his life to God.

It was hot outside but cooler inside the house of God. Casually dressed in pants and a polo shirt, he walked halfway down the aisle and quietly took a seat alone, in a pew on the left side, not far from the confessional booths. Catholic priests were bound to honor the sanctity of the confession, even if a penitent confessed to a mortal sin like murder—or a string of murders.

Eddie was a new but devout parishioner. He listened intently to the service, including the portion called the Eucharistic Sacrifice, during which, the faithful believed, bread and wine were transformed into the body and blood of Jesus Christ.

After mass, the thin silver-haired pastor, Father Sean O'Malley* went to the front of the church and spoke to his parishioners, as they filed out. Eddie patiently waited his turn behind other churchgoers and greeted the kindly Father O'Malley in a quiet, respectful voice.

"You should really preach on the Bible," Eddie, a student of the Old Testament, who carried a Protestant Bible, told the clergyman. Father O'Malley, whose homilies were based upon the New Testament, smiled politely.

"That's true, we really should. That's a good point," he said to the young man, who did not give his name.

Walking the six blocks back to his apartment in the growing summer heat, Eddie passed drug dealers, the killers on the corners, already out and doing business on the Lord's Day.

There were Zodiac wanted posters all over the place, put up by gangs of Guardian Angels. Like Eddie, the subway vigilantes were into karate, wore combat boots and commando berets, and had pledged to fight evil—like the drug dealers and crackheads taking over Eddie's building. Two people had recently died together from a heroin overdose in a nearby apartment.

Eddie had repented his sins to God and cleansed his soul and so should they.

Back in his room, Eddie looked again at the Zodiac coverage in the *Post*, including the "BE READY FOR MORE" front page. In one story, it said a California man identified by police as a prime suspect in the original killings had died in 1992 without being charged. Zodiac was dead? He hadn't seen that anywhere before. The cops had set up another Zodiac Task Force, but if they had been working hard enough, they would have already caught Zodiac.

Eddie turned on his television and found a television preacher preaching the Bible. After his arrest and miraculous release, Eddie had started watching the televangelists because he was curious about why he did the terrible things he was never charged with. Earth, the preacher said, is only a waiting room for heaven. The kingdom of heaven is open to all.

Eddie had repented, which was a very peaceful feeling, but he still bought his gun and commando magazines. He still had his arsenal of weapons, including a long .410-gauge shotgun with a wooden stock. Of course, he no longer had the .22-caliber zip gun and the knife he was carrying when he was arrested.

Eddie had not done penance for his sins. In a new issue of one of his magazines, Eddie read about "Double action .45 combat autos, big-bore crime stoppers!" He had cleansed his soul, but still ordered catalogs for guns, laser gunsighting systems, gunpowder, and the Smith & Wesson Academy of personal security training. He remembered an article he had read years before about a soldier of fortune who came home to America, took on the drug dealers in his neighborhood, and got into a big gun battle with them. He was a hero.

As a choir on television sang a familiar hymn, Eddie again vowed to seek forgiveness and redeem himself in the eyes of God. He vowed again to fight crime and sin.

Onward, Christian soldier.

Chapter 27

ORION THE HUNTER

LOUIE stopped going on hunting trips upstate because he found hunting humans much more satisfying. When you were done hunting a beast of the forest, you had a dead animal. When you were done hunting a human criminal, you had a live bad guy. You had a killer in a cage.

You had justice.

When he saw the new Zodiac letter with the Zodiac happy face and the NYPD sad face, Detective Louie Savarese got angry. He had been waiting for the serial killer to strike again and, now that he had, he couldn't wait to put the sad face on Zodiac.

In subject interrogations, Louie was often cast as the "bad cop," because of his imposing size, shape, and personality. The tattoos that covered his body were hidden by his suit and his Harley-Davidson was in his garage, but Louie was still an arresting figure—with hunter's eyes. Sometimes, he didn't even have to use his booming, bass voice. Another detective remembered that all it took to get a confession out of one particular perp was for "Big Louie" to lumber into the room, stand over the seated suspect, and glare intensely at him. The guy withered under Louie's hard gaze, and immediately confessed to the other, kindly "good cop" detective.

Despite his tough-guy looks, Louie was a gentle giant,

and a family man. His wife, Mary Ann, called him "Big Bear" when no one else was listening. Mary Ann was looking forward to their silver wedding anniversary in a few years, so she could light candles on a cake iced with letters that spelled out the maximum sentence for murder—"twenty-five years to life."

Assigned to the second Zodiac Task Force, Big Louie worked along with two other hero detectives there—Detective Sergeant Joey Herbert and Detective Tommy Maher—who caught Zodiac fever from him. Like their fellow investigators on the task force, the trio worked around the clock. Humor, like their nicknames for each other, relieved some of the tension.

Joey Herbert, thirty-seven, had an oval, baby face surrounded by neatly trimmed sandy hair. Next to Louie, he seemed small and his gentle voice seemed like a whisper. Joey got the nickname "Porkchop," due to his alleged fondness for a good meal. Almost a decade earlier, on December 7, 1983, Joey and a partner were chasing a robbery suspect in Brooklyn when the fleeing felon wheeled around with a knife and stabbed the other officer, wounding him in the face. Joey pulled his gun and fired once, before the man with the knife could plunge the blade into his partner again. The bullet struck the twenty-five-year-old man in the chest, killing him instantly.

Hollywood cop movies give the public the impression that cops who shoot and kill bad guys make catchy, sarcastic remarks, and then romance a partially clothed bimbo. In the real world, the gravity of taking a human life deeply affects cops who are forced to do it. Cops who kill—no matter what the justification—went to the hospital to be treated for trauma.

After the shooting, Joey went to the hospital, and then home to his wife, Barbara, a nurse, who helped him live with what had happened.

Tommy Maher, forty, was a highly decorated detective with fifteen years on the job. He was usually smiling, as if he was enjoying a joke he hadn't told you yet. Occasionally, he sported a baseball cap emblazoned with a cross-and-circle Zodiac Symbol, bearing the words "75th Precinct—Home of the Zodiac Killer." He had two nicknames—one he didn't mind and one he did. He had no problem with "Merciless Maher," because he got it with his ability to smile and joke with a suspect, until the bad guy befriended him—and then he would relentlessly convince his new friend to confess. Tommy was not fond of his other nickname, "Penguin." It implied an undignified resemblance to the flightless bird, due to his prominent nose and five-foot-six-inch stature. When Louie needled him, Tommy would ridicule the bigger man's appearance. "Look at you—you're a bug eater," Tommy would grin. Tommy, the father of four kids, had a good sense of humor—but not because his job experience had been all fun and games. On March 25, 1983, Tommy and several other cops were chasing an eighteen-year-old truck hijacking suspect through the Cypress Hills section when their quarry whipped out a gun and shot Tommy in the left thigh. Tommy, who had already been decorated nine times, wrestled the man who shot him to the ground.

The second Zodiac Task Force had fewer detectives and was headquartered at the 107th Precinct station house in the Fresh Meadows section of Queens. The new Task Force included such detectives as Lieutenant Vincent Mazziotti, Ed Sloan, and Dennis Brooks, who "caught" the original Fonti homicide. Tommy Maher was happy to see that everybody knew what everybody else was doing—and there were no leaks to the press. It was time to get down to business. The calls from tipsters who thought they knew who Zodiac was began pouring in and the work began piling up. Many detectives never believed there were two guys and thought it was the same guy as soon as they saw the "Sleep my little dead" letter.

"Holy shit, our guy's back," was one typical response. On the other hand, perhaps all this talk about two Zodiacs might tempt the killer into an indiscretion, like another letter to the *Post* or a phone call—to protest and take credit.

But there was no word. Why? Was he dead? Did he commit suicide? Was he in a mental hospital, or jail, or was he just careful? Getting down to cases, the investigators began to dig into the mountain of past case files. They reinvestigated and eliminated past suspects while they were hunting for new ones. Some of the first and second Zodiac Task Force members thought the first investigation got "lost in space" with all the arcane astrological and occult mumbo-jumbo. They felt Zodiac was not a ten-foot-tall wizard, but a sneaky mutt—who was difficult to catch only because there was no motive for the shootings and no apparent connection between him and his victims. He would be caught, they felt, with a little luck and a lot of old-fashioned hard work and shoe leather— not by reading tea leaves.

One of the first orders of business was to get the slug out of Jim Weber's thigh and under a microscope. It was the only possible piece of ballistic evidence from the Zodiac II string of shootings. If the round in Weber was in good enough condition for a ballistics examination, the Task Force might know whether it was dealing with one or two shooters.

The shot that hit Diane Ballard had splintered, making it useless. A complete, nondeformed projectile was needed for ballistics testing. The Joseph Diacone round was a through-and-through wound and it was gone. It kept going after exiting his throat and may have continued into the cemetery and buried itself in the hallowed ground. No bullets were found inside the Fonti body and exhumation for a follow-up autopsy was impossible—she had been cremated.

The good news was that, after more than a year inside Jim Weber's thigh muscle, the bullet was still in good shape. It had not hit any bones in its journey from his buttocks to his leg, and was not misshapen. The bad news was that it was a .22-caliber—not a .38, or 9-millimeter, as in the first set of Zodiac attacks. It could not have been fired from the same weapon. But there was one final piece of good news—the smaller slug was just as smooth as previous Zodiac bullets. There were no lands and grooves, which made it consistent with the larger-caliber Zodiac rounds. It was still possible a copycat was at work, but—because so few smooth bullets were found—it was much more likely it was the same guy, using a similar weapon of a different caliber. He probably had a collection of homemade zip guns, or a collection of antique firearms. More than seven thousand slugs had been tested by the NYPD lab the previous year, but only twenty of them, or .03 percent of those bullets, had no grooves or markings. All zip guns and weapons seized by police without spiral grooves inside the barrel would be tested and compared to the bullets that had killed Joe Proce and wounded Jim Weber.

A high priority of the Task Force was investigating past arrests or seizures of zip guns and smooth-bore weapons. Louie began hunting in police records for "zips"—zip-gun arrests from East New York, Cypress Hills, and Highland Park in Brooklyn and Woodhaven, Queens. He came up with 175 of them, all of which had to be typed onto a separate DD-5 report. He submitted the stack of reports that requested handwriting checks with the Documents Section, and fingerprint comparisons by the Zodiac fingerprint specialist, Detective Ronnie Alongis at the Latent Prints section at One Police Plaza. No prints matched, but about thirty percent came back denied—due to sealed arrest records. Fingerprints were not available. In the absence of other compelling factors, that effectively ended investigation of those suspects.

One of the forty or so names that was denied was preserved in Louie's handwritten notebook entry of December 9, 1994: "Heriberto Seda, 2730 Pitkin." Police records showed Seda had been busted five months previously, with a zip gun that didn't work. The charges had been dropped and he had no previous arrest record. No one had ever reported him to police, or either Task Force, as a Zodiac suspect.

He was a ghost.

Despite the fact that his fingerprints were not the ones on the 1990 Zodiac letters, George Gold became a Zodiac suspect again. Some detectives from the first Task Force couldn't give up on Gold and again placed him under surveillance. When they observed him relieving himself in a particular alley one night, one of the more bizarre episodes of an already bizarre case began. Investigators once more applied Chief Borrelli's dictum, that, if it wasn't illegal or immoral, and they thought it might work—why not give it a try?

An undercover operation was launched to retrieve a quantity of George Gold's urine, for comparison to the DNA sample obtained from the saliva on the flap of the envelope sent by Zodiac to the *Post* in 1990. Like the garbage collection operation four years earlier, it wasn't illegal, it wasn't immoral, but it was going to be smelly.

Detectives, carrying materials to absorb and preserve fluid, followed Gold for weeks. One night, Gold again entered the same alley and the operation went into high gear. The suspect deposited the evidence in the alley and left, unaware that a team of detectives was waiting to pounce on it. The innovative investigators got their man's urine—but, alas, there was no DNA match. Even after the noble failure, some determined detectives maintained that there was no "hit" because Zodiac could have had someone else lick the letter. Gold remained a suspect.

Arrest records of literally anyone busted in the Seven-Five Precinct were checked and their fingerprints were compared to the Zodiac Killer, without results. Next, detectives created "The Grid"—a huge, eighty-five-block area surrounding Highland Park. The grid stretched from the park and the graveyards, south to Atlantic Avenue, west to Pennsylvania Avenue, and east to Euclid Avenue. Acting on the probable age of Zodiac in the police psychological profile, city records were checked for men of all races between the ages of twenty-nine and fifty-four living inside the grid. They came up with an astronomical forty-five hundred male residents—all potential Zodiac suspects. Every name had to be laboriously typed by hand onto a DD-5 report, requesting an arrest record and fingerprint check. If a man who lived in the neighborhood had ever been arrested, his print file went to Detective Ronnie Alongis at headquarters for comparison and elimination.

The operation took months. It was a gargantuan undertaking, one worthy of a giant like Orion the Hunter himself—the paper equivalent of a house-to-house search for Zodiac.

It didn't work.

Joey Herbert had been through a lot in thirteen years on the job, but he told his colleagues that notifying Patricia Fonti's young son that his mother was dead was one of the most depressing days of his life.

"It was the hardest thing I ever had to do. It was the saddest day of my life," Joey said.

Victim Joseph Diacone had no family that would claim him. His remains went into a pauper's grave in Potter's Field, the city burial grounds on Hart Island. Prisoners from nearby Riker's Island dug the mass graves and lined the wooden coffins inside in rows for interment.

Despite a massive investigation, and months of work that turned up a few more possible Zodiac suspects, there was never a "hit" on the prints, the gun, or the DNA. The second Zodiac Task Force went the way of the first and was disbanded. Detective Ray Liebold had retired and the troubling and frustrating Zodiac case went to Detective Ed Sloan and his boss, Detective Lieutenant Vincent Mazziotti, who became the keepers of the Zodiac flame in Queens.

Tommy, Joey, and Louie made a pact that they would never stop hunting for the Zodiac. The trio of detectives shared a belief that Zodiac was still in East New York, biding his time, and they were determined to get him, Task Force or not.

Tommy never expected to catch the Z-man personally, but he thought if the killer was ever caught, it would be in the Seven-Five.

Joey had an amazing capacity for detail. He knew every detail of every shooting. He memorized all of the Zodiac letters and kept poring over his copies, even at home, look-ing for some detail that he had missed, something that might be important. How did Zodiac form the different letters? Was he left-handed or right-handed? What words did he capitalize? Which ones did he underline? How many times? What did it mean? Joey began buying books on serial killings and pattern criminals. He read every book on serial killers that he could find. Books like *Hunting Humans* were in every room of his house. His wife found her husband's interest a bit strange, but he was trying to find out where Zodiac was coming from, what made him tick. Joey knew serial killers didn't just stop—Zodiac had simply gone to ground. He was hibernating. He knew the killer was out there and he was coming back. Joey couldn't let it go. With the Task Force folding, he decided to ex-pand his horizons and sign up for a Hostage Negotiation course.

They were all convinced Zodiac was going to strike again and was just waiting for things to get quiet again, like an animal hiding in a thicket. They went back to their regular detective work, but would systematically check every shooting in the city, looking for a Zodiac connection.

After a great meal in Chinatown one night, Louie drove his wife, Mary Ann, and their three sons, Louie Jr., Wyatt, and Lyle, to East New York. After dessert and fortune cookies, Louie took his family on a guided tour of Zodiac Killer murder sites, because his family wanted to see what had been obsessing him, keeping him away from home and giving him sleepless nights. Highland Park was an unlikely spot for a family outing for a detective and his family from the suburbs. That night, Mary Ann noticed Louie was having another one of his Zodiac nightmares, tossing and turning and talking to himself in the dark.

Louie was hunting Zodiac in his dreams.

Chapter 28

DOING GOD'S WORK

CHACHI thought her brother Eddie was getting stranger. He seemed like a different person on different days. One day, he would be calm and quiet, and pray and watch television in his room. The next day, he would be intense and angry, the rage coming off him like a smell. He even looked like a different person. She had dropped out of high school at sixteen, and was working behind the counter of a local bakery. Chachi was still cute, but she had gained a lot of weight, perhaps as a result of too much free pastry. She still had smooth, mocha-colored skin, and dreamy brown eyes. Chachi was, in many ways, the opposite of her half brother—friendly, quick to laugh, and anxious to have friends and be liked. Hers was the only earned paycheck coming into the household. She felt she had ambition, unlike her lazy brother—who wouldn't walk across the street to apply for welfare. Eddie lectured her on sin. She felt he was simply jealous of her love life, since he didn't have any.

One of her customers at the bakery was a nice old Spanish guy with a limp. As she wrapped and rang up his baked goods, he would smile and chat pleasantly with her, while leaning on a wooden cane with a carved handle.

Chachi never asked his name, and Mario Orozco, the first Zodiac shooting victim, never gave it.

In March of 1995, Eddie approached Seven-Five Precinct uniformed Officer Kathleen Vigiano outside his building and told her there was a woman selling drugs in his building. Vigiano, a nine-year veteran with long blond hair, began watching the building and noticed a pattern of apparent drug-sales activity. She started doing "vertical patrols," in the building, which was a police term for walking up stairs, checking the roof, and walking back down again. On one of her patrols, several months later, she saw a young woman standing on the second-floor landing. When the cop asked her what she was doing in the building, the woman said she had been visiting a friend. After speaking to the cop, she quickly left the building. Once the woman had gone, the red door of Apartment 10 on the floor above swung open.

"That's the girl selling drugs in here," Eddie told Vigiano. "She hides her drugs in the windowsill."

The officer found a black bag containing a few "decks" of heroin—glassine envelopes used to package the white powder. She confiscated the dope.

A few days later the policewoman came back and found the same woman standing on the third-floor landing, right outside Eddie's door. When asked why she was there, the woman pointed to the red door and said she was visiting a friend there. The cop knocked on the door and Eddie, dressed in black, as always, opened it. Eddie told Vigiano he did not know the woman.

Vigiano told the woman to move from where she was standing, and the cop saw several drug packets on the floor.

"You're under arrest," said Vigiano, who handcuffed the woman's hands behind her back. The arrested woman glared at Eddie, with a vengeful look known on the street as "later-for-you."

Eddie was elated. It was the first arrest of his new mission. From reading his books on serial killers, Eddie knew that Ted Bundy had been a good citizen, too, a hero. In

1969, Bundy earned a police commendation for capturing a purse snatcher. That same year, he rescued a three-year-old child from drowning in a Seattle, Washington, lake. Bundy was also a volunteer at a crisis clinic hot line, where the killer helped troubled callers. The sadistic rapist and murderer even wrote a pamphlet for women on rape prevention.

Eddie had been a ghost in the neighborhood. Most residents had never seen him, but he suddenly became known as a rat with a Bible. In case there was any doubt about his identity, he took his blue Bible to the dope corners and preached on the sinful evils of drugs to the dealers themselves. His mission was to rid his building and the neighborhood of drug dealers. The cops couldn't do it, the federal government couldn't do it, but Eddie was going to try. Was it a suicide mission, did Eddie want to go out as a hero—blown away by the bad guys?

In Chachi's little corner of the living room, she had her desk and television and stereo and books. She was fascinated with the Mafia and read any book on the mob she could find. Against the wishes of her mother and brother, Chachi hung out on the corner. The teen liked laughing and dancing and there wasn't much of that at home. It was a lot more fun with her friends on the corner, where she could hear the bouncing, booming sounds of Salsa music and smell the mouth-watering aromas of frying food from nearby Latino restaurants. She was popular in the neighborhood, had a series of boyfriends, and knew all the local drug dealers and "gangstas." She had made it clear to her friends that she didn't like her brother, that she thought he was crazy.

"That motherfucker never does nothin' but sit in that room," she said. "I'm breakin' my ass workin' to bring some money in and he tell me I can't bring my friends in the house."

One member of a local drug crew, a young businessman

by the name of Yo-Yo,* approached her with a friendly warning:

"Yo, Chachi, why's yo brothuh always nosey for? I was gonna blow up yo house, 'causa yo brothuh, but I like you."

Yo-Yo's message was clear. She had to shut her brother's mouth. If she didn't, she and her mother had better start sleeping on the floor, where they were less likely to get hit by the hail of bullets that would some night explode into the apartment, looking for Eddie.

At five-foot-seven-inches tall, Chachi was only one inch shorter than her brother, but she now outweighed him by twenty pounds. Chachi passed on Yo-Yo's message, with interest.

"Yo, stay out of these motherfuckers' business," she told Eddie. "You always in other people's business. Stay out of it. I know all these guys. You don't stay out they business, they gonna murder yo' ass. They tol' me they gonna blow up the house. I don't want my house blown up by a gang—'cause you gotta keep opening your mouth to cops."

"It's God's business. I'm doing God's work," Eddie said calmly.

"Yo, I hope they kill yo ass," said an infuriated Chachi, walking away.

Eddie told his new friend, Officer Vigiano, about stores on Pitkin Avenue that were selling drugs from behind the counter. Vigiano reported the tip to the office of the Brooklyn District Attorney, who arranged for plainclothes narcotics officers to make two undercover drug "buys" of marijuana. Based upon the drug purchases, a search warrant was obtained. Cops raided one store, a block from Eddie's apartment, and confiscated two hundred bags of "chronic," as the illegal weed was called on the street. Four men were brought out in handcuffs.

Eddie had been warned by his sister to lay off and mind his own business, and he had ignored the warning. Drug dealers did not sue—they settled out of court. Several men pounced on him one day outside his building and gave him a sound beating with fists and feet, accompanied by threats. He would not get another warning.

In the spring of 1996, Vigiano told Eddie that she would no longer be on foot patrol, but would soon start bike patrol elsewhere in the neighborhood. She thought Eddie seemed relaxed and fairly intelligent. Vigiano, the mother of two young children, thanked Eddie for his help and good citizenship and asked the obvious question.

"Why are you helping me? Don't you have a job?"

"I'm doing God's work," said Eddie. "There's a lot of evil on these streets and that's why I help cops with drug dealers."

Vigiano asked if Eddie went to church. He said he attended Saint Fortunata's.

"I go every Sunday, Don't you?"

"Yes, I do." Vigiano lied. She said she attended church regularly, because Eddie seemed very serious. She didn't want to alienate the snitch.

"Why don't you move out?"

"I can't, I live with my mother." Eddie told her that he was very concerned about his sister and did not like her behavior.

"I do not like little sister hanging around with drug dealers," he said.

During a lull in the conversation, Eddie changed the subject.

"Remember the Zodiac case?"

Vigiano said she did.

"Did they ever make an arrest? Did they ever get anybody for that?"

Vigiano said she wasn't sure, but she didn't think so.

"Do they have any leads, did they ever have any suspects?"

She said she didn't know. She hadn't been involved in the investigation and had not been in the precinct while it was going on. Vigiano encouraged him to get his high school equivalency diploma and gave him a phone number to call to sign up for classes.

Back in his room, Eddie put aside the number Officer Vigiano had given him, and resumed work on the second pipe bomb. He also had a canister of tear gas, and a small homemade hand grenade. They would come in handy if the drug dealers came after him again.

He had not yet decided where he would detonate his bombs. Maybe he would explode them in Manhattan, in the subway at rush hour?

Chapter 29

SHOOTING STARS

a

GLADYS Alvarado drank her morning coffee from her golden "Gladys" mug. On the white refrigerator, held to the door by a magnet, was a month-old Mother's Day card signed "Heriberto," who drew a happy face next to his name. Next to the card hung a fat, blood-red satin heart with "I Love You, Mom," printed on it—from Chachi. Despite the sentiments from them, Gladys knew things were not right with her children. Eddie was in his room, praying aloud and preaching to himself. Chachi would probably go and hang out on the corner with those street people, instead of finishing high school.

June 18, 1996, was a beautiful, sunny day. It was already hot when Gladys walked out of the building to the corner subway to take the train to Manhattan to attend the Spanish-language mass at Saint Patrick's Cathedral, as she did every day.

After his morning prayers, Eddie resumed reading *Black Rainbow*, a Barbara Michaels Gothic ghost novel set in England in 1854. It was filled with lustful pagan ceremonies and sacrifices. The cover illustration was of a woman's marble tomb from the Middle Ages. The female heroine was employed by an odd man named Edmund. She herself was a very strange young lady, who, "Under the spell of the black rainbow . . . remembered things she would rather have forgotten . . .'' In the book, eerie nights were perfect ''for Diana, the huntress, whose other persona is the witch goddess Hecate, and whose pack hunts human prey.''

On two of his recent forays into the outside world, Eddie had lost control. The previous week, someone bumped into him in front of the building. Eddie exploded into a rage, shouting obscenities and shoving people.

''I'm going to start killing! I'm going to start killing motherfuckers because I'm not getting no sex!''

Eddie put down the black Gothic novel. It was hard to concentrate. There were reminders everywhere. The papers were full of stories about the capture of the Unabomber serial bomber and a local serial killer named Royster, who had just confessed. They both made the front page of the *Post* and the other papers. Eddie had that feeling again. It was getting harder and harder to stay in control. He had to pray, to resist lust and evil impulses. He picked up his blue Bible.

From the back bedroom of Gladys's apartment—the room with the blue roses—came the voice of a man praying. The prayers were interrupted by a guttural voice that snarled obscenities.

''Fuck you! Fuck everybody!''

Outside, it was a ''sunny, sunny day'' and, hidden by the noontime sun, the daystars were shining brightly overhead, like in Joe Proce's poem. Beyond the bright blue sky, the Seven Sisters were almost overhead in the southwest. Orion the Hunter, with his club, was close behind. Leo the Lion was slinking away toward the horizon.

After mass at Saint Patrick's Cathedral, Gladys went to one of the smaller altar shrines and lit flickering candles inside red glass holders for her children. In the quiet of the cathedral, Gladys looked, not to herself for strength, but to God. Eddie had repented after he was arrested with a gun, but nothing had changed. Chachi was also on the wrong path, hanging out with street people. Gladys wanted it to stop. She knelt on the cool marble and rested her elbows on the brass railing. She closed her eyes and put her hands together in prayer. As she had so many times before, she asked that her children be given power, the strength to do what they had to do.

While her mother was out, Chachi got a call from a friend and invited him over. Wilbur Rios, 23, was nicknamed "Tush," which rhymed with push. He had an extensive criminal record and was clad in trendy designer casual wear, from head to foot. He wore designer jeans, a large, white "Pelle" T-shirt and a blue Tommy Hilfiger baseball cap. Tush, who had a number of aliases, had been arrested for selling drugs, for robbery and reckless endangerment. When he arrived, he and Chachi went into her bedroom.

Chachi and Wilbur were laughing. Eddie didn't like laughing like that. It was sinful. They were going to do something that only married people should do. Eddie began banging on the wall his room shared with his sister's bedroom.

"What's the matter with your brother?" Tush asked.

"I don't know."

Chachi knew perfectly well that when Eddie thumped the wall with his fists, it meant the stranger had to get out of the apartment immediately. She had never ignored his warning before. Eddie pounded on the wall over and over. Chachi ignored him and the pounding stopped.

Bang!

Eddie threw a shot through his white wooden door. It flew across the living room and bored into the kitchen wall.

"What the fuck?" Chachi shouted. She wasn't scared of Eddie anymore, she was mad. She jumped off the bed, and stormed through Eddie's door.

"What the fuck is wrong with you?"

Eddie was standing calmly in the middle of his room

with his arms folded across his chest. His eyes were dark, looking up from under black, arched brows. His right hand was hidden under his left armpit. A crooked smile was fixed on his face.

"Why you always in my business?" Chachi shouted. "Why the fuck you always gotta get in my business? Stay the fuck out of my business. What I do is my business, it shouldn't concern you. If you do that again . . ."

"If I do that again, what?" asked her sneering brother.

"What the fuck is wrong with you? Fuck you, motherfucker!" Chachi screamed. As she spun around to leave, she heard Eddie yell back at her, "Fuck you!"

She never saw him whip up the .410-gauge shotgun he had been holding under his arm. Eddie fired. The gun went off like a bomb.

Boom!

Chachi felt like she was hit in the butt and knocked down by something hot. Her nerves were on fire. She fell facedown on the wooden floor and then scrambled to her feet.

"Tush! Tush! Tush! Help me, I'm shot!" Chachi screamed. Her back was burning. She touched it with her right hand and felt blood pouring out. There was blood everywhere. Tush hid behind the bedroom door.

"Help!" She stumbled through the living room and into the kitchen. Eddie was right behind her. She grabbed the cordless phone off the wall and was only able to dial a nine and a one before Eddie slapped it from her hand. He ripped the entire base unit out of the wall and threw it onto the floor, smashing it.

Chachi collapsed onto the floor, crying, her blood smearing across the spotless white linoleum as she tried to crawl away.

Eddie stood over his helpless sister, but was distracted by something behind him. He ran back into the living room to threaten Tush, who was looking out of Chachi's bedroom door.

"Get back in that room before I kill you!" Eddie shouted.

Tush ducked back into the room and madly began piling furniture against the inside of the door. Eddie moved toward his own room.

He's going to get another gun, Chachi thought. He's berserk. He's going to murder me. She scrambled to her feet and staggered out the door. She banged on the door of her neighbor.

"Please help me! It's Chachi!" The peephole opened, but not the door. "Open the door! Please help me! I'm hurt," she begged, holding up her bloody hand. "Please let me in!" She began to pray. The door opened. The woman admitted Chachi, who collapsed on her couch. The woman quickly locked the door and went to get towels to soak up the blood. Her four children turned away from the television screen and stared at the girl bleeding on their couch.

"God, don't take me now," Chachi prayed out loud. She was dizzy and her legs were numb. She wiggled her feet to make sure she wasn't paralyzed, while her neighbor called police. Chachi felt herself losing consciousness.

"I'm dying," she thought.

It was ten minutes after noon. Two paramedics soon arrived and began trying to save Chachi's life. They got there before the cops.

Seven-Five Precinct Bike Patrol Officer Dale Schultz, 29, had only been on two-wheeled patrol for five minutes when he heard a "10-34" job over his radio. It was a "confirmed, female shot" inside 2730 Pitkin, just two blocks away. As he pedaled the two blocks, the radio said two Emergency Medical Service paramedics had already arrived and were inside, treating the victim. It sounded like everything was over. Schultz turned his bike around and sped to the scene. When he arrived at the courtyard of the building a few minutes later, he saw that two transit police officers had emerged from the nearby subway and were just about to enter the dirty, old brick building.

"He's still in here!" someone shouted. The cops looked up. The outburst, apparently from Wilbur in Chachi's bedroom, ruined the element of surprise for Eddie, who leaned out the kitchen window and pointed one of his guns down on the cops.

Boom!

Schultz and the other officers jumped at the noise, which sounded like a cannon in the enclosed courtyard. The pavement at the cops' feet chipped and exploded with cement dust from the shot. It came from a third-floor window, where there was a puff of white smoke. All three cops were already running back toward the street. All they knew was somebody was shooting at them, trying to kill them, and they were like fish in a barrel.

Boom!

The shot ricocheted off the sidewalk right behind the cops. Schultz dove head-first over the hood of a car at the curb and landed in the street. His right elbow and knee were bruised, scraped, and bleeding, but Schultz didn't notice. A thirty-year-old man walking on the sidewalk was struck with a piece of flying masonry, which cut his neck.

Boom!

The shot slammed into the car, just as Schultz scrambled behind it, lying on his stomach on the hot concrete of Pitkin Avenue. He grabbed his radio and issued a distress call.

"Ten-thirteen! Shots being fired at police officers!" Schultz yelled into his radio. The radio code 10–13, "officer needs assistance," was the most urgent police radio message.

Boom!

Schultz saw the shot hit a car that the two transit cops had taken cover behind. Incredibly, he saw civilians walking around on the block, looking curiously at the noise. He yelled at them to get away. Men and women scattered.

Several people grabbed children and carried them down into the subway station on the corner, to escape the gunfire.

Boom!

A shot chipped up pavement in the middle of the street.

Schultz crawled on his stomach behind the row of parked cars, until he was out of the line of fire. He dashed to the front of the building and hugged the brick wall on his right. He pulled out his .38-caliber handgun, walked to the corner of the courtyard, and went down on the sidewalk on one knee, ready to fire. He peeked around the corner to the right. In the third-floor window, he saw a dark-haired man, leaning out and looking to his right, toward him. The man saw Schultz and pointed something at him.

Boom!

Schultz saw a bright muzzle flash from the weapon and a blast of gunsmoke. As he pulled his head back in, the shot hit the corner of the building by his head. Chips of brick and red dust sprayed past him.

An unmarked police car roared into the block, lights flashing and siren wailing, the police equivalent of the Seventh Cavalry. It screeched to a stop on Pitkin Avenue, across the street from the building. Two cops got out and were immediately pinned down behind cars by the gunfire.

Boom! Boom!

One of the new arrivals squatted behind the Emergency Medical Service ambulance, but his partner, a husky six-foot-four cop, was caught in the open. He dove into the street and tried to fit his entire body behind the engine block of a compact car. Another car arrived and three young uniformed cops from the Warrants Squad jumped out, guns in hand. More reinforcements.

Schultz grabbed his gun with both hands. He wanted to let this guy know he was still there. He wanted to get him to stop shooting at the cops behind the cars. He took a deep breath, swung his gun around the corner, and aimed it up at the window.

The guy wasn't there. Schultz waited, his heart pounding, keeping his gun trained on the window. As soon as the guy poked his head out, he squeezed the trigger.

Bang! Bang! Bang! Bang!

The gunman ducked back inside. Did he get him? The shooter appeared again in the window, taking aim again. Schultz ducked back behind the brick wall.

Across the street, Officer Bill Schub, twenty-six, was about to step into the street, when his partner yelled a warning and dove for the pavement.

"Look out!"

Boom!

More masonry chips and redbrick dust flew past Schultz's head. Across the street, Schub saw a muzzle flash and a puff of smoke. He brought his own gun up and fired.

Bang!

Bang! Bang! Bang!

The cop behind the ambulance also fired back at the gunman. Schub ducked behind a parked truck. His partner and the other cop also had taken cover. Schub, who was wearing his bulletproof vest, stepped out from behind the truck. He was looking down the shining barrel of a large gun, aimed right at him from across the street.

Boom!

The lead whizzed past Schub and ricocheted with a crack off something behind him. Too close. He ducked back under cover.

Schultz was upset to see that his backup, his rescuers, were pinned down by the withering fire. The sniper had the high ground. He grabbed his radio again.

"Central, don't have any units come to the front of 2730 Pitkin, shots still being fired." Schultz noticed Officer Suzanne Johnson come up behind him, with her pistol in her hand. At that point, there were at least nine cops who were either under fire or pinned down in the street by the sniper. The big cop behind the small car brought his gun up to return fire, but didn't shoot. He was afraid of hitting the people leaning out of other windows in the gunman's building. Despite the flying lead, they were trying to see what was happening, or were pointing to the shooter's window.

Boom!

The gunman blasted at the street again. Lead pelted the pavement near one of the pinned-down officers. The shooter was trading shot for shot with the cops. The officers kept their heads down. Schultz asked for backup from the ESU, Emergency Services Unit, what some departments around the country called the SWAT team. The cops who were pinned down had to keep yelling at people who were trying to walk down the block during the raging gun battle.

"Get down! Get back! Get back!" the big cop behind the small car shouted to one little old lady, who refused to leave until he screamed at her.

"Just another day in East New York," the cop said to himself.

Eddie had lost control. The anger kept on flowing out of him, in hot waves. He didn't try to control it anymore. It just kept on going, kept on flowing. He put on his Swiss Army helmet and bobbed in and out of the kitchen window over the plants, firing and reloading, firing and reloading. There were guns and bullets and pipe bombs all over Gladys's kitchen table. Her happy kitchen smelled like a firing range. A couple of cops' bullets crashed into the apartment but missed Eddie. Every time a cop stuck up his head or fired, Eddie fired back. He was winning. While he was reloading, he heard yelling from the back of the apartment. He ran to his room and heard a voice coming from outside—it was his neighbor next door. She was yelling to somebody outside about his sister. He heard men's voices in the rear yard below. Cops.

*   *   *

Scores of cops arrived and blocked off a nine-block area around the gun battle. Heavy reinforcements were on the way—including helicopters and "the tank," a blue-and-white armored vehicle. Subway service to the Euclid Avenue stop was halted and kids at two nearby schools were rushed inside. A uniformed three-man anti-burglary team, Officers Bill Mincher, twenty-nine, and his partner, Keith Casey, twenty-seven, along with Paul Corr, thirty, arrived and joined other cops in a move to surround the building and enter it from the rear.

They ran around the corner, down Euclid Avenue, and vaulted a chain-link fence. They were joined by a sergeant and three other cops. Residents were fleeing down the fire escape. A man who scrambled out one window and down the rear fire escape was grabbed and handcuffed because the officers did not know if he was the gunman, an accomplice, or a resident of the building.

"It's not me! It's not me! I live here!" the terrified man yelled, as he was taken away for questioning.

A hysterical woman stuck her head out a third-floor window, atop the black metal fire escape, and yelled down to cops.

"His sister's shot in the back! Shot in the back!" It was Chachi's helpful neighbor. She, Chachi, her children, and the two paramedics were trapped in her apartment, helplessly listening to the gun battle next door.

"Where is he?" one cop shouted.

"Who shot her?" said another. The woman suddenly vanished, without another word.

Mincher, Casey, and Corr pulled down the noisy ladder to the fire escape. Mincher was about to climb up, and had his foot on the bottom rung, when a man stuck his head out of a third-floor window above.

Boom! The gun blast from above was earsplitting.

Lead hit the pavement in between the three cops—right at their feet. Concrete chips flew everywhere. They jumped for cover, but there wasn't any. At least three cops, in-

cluding Mincher and Casey, landed, crouching, under a fire
escape, with their backs against the wall of the building.
Some cops were praying to themselves, some were cursing
out loud. Some were doing both. They were all sweating
heavily in the heat. The fire escape above them was half
metal and half air, with a small blanket spread out on the
lowest landing. The other three cops landed on their feet,
squeezed together in a small basement doorway, pressed
against a metal door—trying to become two-dimensional.

Boom! Another shot hit the pavement.

"What the fuck's going on here?" shouted one cop.

"Where is he?" shouted another. "Can you see him?"

Boom!

"Holy fuck, what the fuck is going on here?"

"Who's shooting?"

Corr was jammed into the tiny doorway—with Sergeant
David Rosen on one side and Officer Mike Wallen on the
other. Wallen's right hand was stuck awkwardly over his
head, his gun pointing upwards. Rosen was outwardly cool
under fire and called for assistance calmly on his radio.
The radio dispatcher, dealing with the officers pinned
down in front, did not immediately realize the urgency of
the situation and told them to stand by.

Boom!

The hot lead clanged as it hit the metal of the fire escape,
and ricocheted off, before it could hit the cops.

"Check yourselves. Is everybody okay?" Rosen asked.

Boom!

"Tell them we're trapped back here!" one cop yelled
to Rosen. Another cop grabbed a radio and called in a
"Ten-Thirteen:

"Central, emergency message—you've got seven cops
pinned down in the back, shots fired." The dispatcher told
the trapped cops that ESU units were on the way.

Boom!

In between the shots fired at them, the officers heard
more firing out front. How many guys were firing?

"Please, God, let this be the last round," Paul Corr prayed to himself, thinking of his wife and young daughter. Corr was trying to become part of the wall of the building, which he had been inside exactly a week before. When he and other officers were there, a man on the third floor opened his red door and spoke to Corr.

"Can I help you?" asked the Hispanic man, who was dressed in black.

"Are there any people using drugs in the building?" Corr asked.

"There's no drug dealers in here. I kicked them all out," he replied. He was dead serious.

Corr, who walked a Zodiac foot post years before, later spoke about the man to Kathleen Vigiano, who told him she knew the guy, who "was like a cross between a vigilante and a religious fanatic." He had no idea the polite, fanatic vigilante was the one trying to blow his head off.

Boom!

Casey and the others had no room to stand up under the fire escape. Their legs were cramping but Mincher warned Casey not to sit down. The ground under them was a carpet of empty crack vials and bloody hypodermic needles. It was raining bullets, their only umbrella was an open fire escape and a blanket, and his partner was warning him not to get AIDS from a needle. It was funny, but Casey was too scared to laugh.

Boom!

The round hit the pavement in front of the fire escape.

"Casey, how's your heart?" Mincher whispered.

"Pounding."

"Mine, too."

It was almost fifteen minutes before the ESU officers arrived. It felt like two hours. They were clad in bullet-proof "POLICE" body armor and helmets and carried "Mini-14" .30-caliber assault rifles. One trained his weapon on the gunman's window and another helmeted cop told the trapped officers they were going to evacuate them.

"All right," said one ESU cop, "we're going to cover you and we're going to take you out one at a time."

The problem was that they would have to run across the open yard, jump a five-foot wall, and run down a side alley to the front of the building—under the gun. It was like an old war movie.

First one officer and then another bolted from the doorway to safety and there was no firing. There were no shots from the front, either. Corr was the last to leave the doorway. He lurched into the open, but his legs turned to rubber, like in a nightmare. He fell flat on his face but scrambled up and sprinted around the corner of the building. All the cops in the rear and out front were successfully evacuated, without further gunplay. The shooter had stopped shooting. The first thing the cops did, after being debriefed, was to call their families—the shoot-out was being carried live on television.

"What is going on in your precinct?" one worried wife asked her husband when he called.

"I'll tell you later," he said.

Detective Sergeant Joey Herbert got the call for his first hostage negotiation and sped to 2730 Pitkin Avenue, along with two other negotiators, Detective Lieutenant Kerry Schriner and Detective Sergeant Kenneth Bowen. After all the officers in the shoot-out had been evacuated, the negotiators suited up in ballistic vests and helmets and were briefed on the situation, in which a gunman named Eddie had shot his sister and barricaded himself inside a third-floor apartment with one male hostage. Joey moved into the courtyard with Emergency Services cops, behind a large rolling metal shield with a thick window, like a bulletproof door on wheels. They did not know that Eddie had bombs. It felt like a hundred degrees in the lifesaving gear. Joey kept his gun in his holster and carried a notebook and pen, to jot down any names or important information. His first goal was simple—get the guy to start talking and stop shooting.

"My name is Joey," he yelled into the courtyard. There was no answer. Joey made an appeal to the guy, whose name was Eddie, to stop the shooting and the bloodshed. He was answered with obscenities. The man seemed irrational.

"Get the cops off the roof! I'm going to start shooting," Eddie yelled a few minutes later.

Schriner had quietly lowered a cellular phone to Wilbur in the front bedroom, and was telling him to remain calm and quiet.

"Get the helicopters out of here!" Eddie screamed. "You guys are bugging me! I have explosives, I'm barricaded!"

Joey responded in calm, measured tones. He told Eddie that his sister "was just shot in the rear end. She's going to be okay. No more bloodshed—I don't want you to get hurt and I don't want to get hurt."

"You're lying to me! Why are all the cops here? Get the cops away!"

Eddie disappeared from the window after each outburst, but kept coming back. He wasn't shooting. He was talking. Forty-five minutes after the dialogue had begun, Joey and the others left the courtyard and entered the front of the building through an apartment window. They went through the apartment, and cautiously up the stairs. The red door on the third floor was half open.

"No more blood, Eddie," Joey shouted to him through the open door.

"I want some time to think," Eddie responded.

Joey asked how Wilbur was doing.

"I'm gonna shoot him," said Eddie.

"We're not going to shoot anybody else," Joey said, and changed the subject. Mostly, Joey said the same things over and over and Eddie listened.

''What time is it?'' Eddie asked suddenly. Joey told him it was three-thirteen in the afternoon.

''Well, listen, I think I will surrender,'' said Eddie. ''How much time am I gonna serve in jail?''

Joey told him that it probably wouldn't be that long, since nobody was dead or anything.

''Which jail am I going to?'' he asked. Eddie said he didn't want to go to Riker's Island. He wanted to go to an upstate correctional facility. Joey told Eddie they were going to lower a bucket for him to put the guns in.

''I have six or seven guns,'' said Eddie. ''I want to unload them first.'' Cops on the roof lowered a bucket outside the kitchen window several times, and Eddie filled it with thirteen guns.

Joey asked about the explosives.

''I have pipe bombs . . . in my room all the way in the back. Two small pipe bombs, a tear-gas canister, and one small grenade. There's a bunch of ammunition in there,'' Eddie answered.

''Joey, I want you to come down with me. You come down with me.''

He agreed to accompany Eddie down to the car. After all the guns were out of the apartment, ESU cops entered the apartment and took Eddie into custody. Joey removed his helmet and vest. It was like he had taken a bath in sweat. Cops released Wilbur from his hiding place and took him away for questioning.

''I should have killed him,'' Eddie said, casually, as he saw Wilbur leave.

Joey escorted Eddie out to the squad car, as he had promised, but he wasn't the arresting officer. Eddie squinted up into the bright afternoon sky. He couldn't see the triumphant Orion the Hunter or the Seven Sisters, but they were there.

Police searching the brightly decorated apartment found a Disneyland of death in Eddie's room. Comic books and kids' toys were found next to more weapons—including nine unfinished pipe bombs, blowguns, a crossbow, and a machete.

Not long after Eddie was driven away, Gladys returned home. She had to walk several blocks, carrying a bag of cleaning products, because the subway would not go to the Euclid Avenue stop. As she got closer to her home, she saw more and more police, until she realized that whatever was happening was going on in her own building. She broke into a run. A neighbor on the first floor greeted her as she ran up.

"What happened?"

"Your daughter got shot. Your son did it. The cops arrested him."

"Oh, my goodness! Chachi! God give me strength!" Gladys was in shock. Her son was in jail and she didn't know whether her daughter Chachi was alive or dead. She took a taxi to Brookdale Hospital.

One of the Seven-Five detectives pressed into service to canvass the neighborhood for witnesses to the shoot-out was Tommy Maher, who heard about the homemade zip guns used by the kid who had surrendered.

"Wouldn't it be a pisser if this was the Z-man?" asked Tommy, with a smile.

Everyone laughed. It was funny.

Chapter 30

THE RUSH

WHEN Eddie was sitting alone, handcuffed, in a room at the Seven-Five Precinct, Officer Kathleen Vigiano walked in and asked him about all the guns he had.

"They're a hobby," Eddie said, with a silky smirk. "I stopped making them when I was a kid."

"Why'd you shoot your sister in the back?"

"I didn't shoot her in the back," Eddie responded angrily. "I shot her. I don't know where I shot her."

"Why were you shooting at cops? I was out there, you could've shot me."

"You were? I didn't see you. I'm sorry."

"Those were my friends out there. You could have shot my friends," said the cop.

"I just shot my sister, and they have guns and I have guns," said Eddie, as if that explained it all.

After a moment, Vigiano asked Eddie if he needed anything.

"Yes. Could I have a glass of water?"

Detective Danny Powers, 33, arrested Eddie Seda for fifteen counts of attempted murder, as well as multiple counts of possession of deadly weapons and explosives. He advised Eddie of his rights. Eddie was polite and cooperative and agreed to give Powers a written confession to the shoot-out.

Eddie knew the cops had him for shooting Chachi and shooting at the cops, but nobody had mentioned Zodiac. Could the magic still be working? Would they let him go again? He would call upon God and pray they would.

At 4:30 P.M., Powers gave Eddie a pen and a legal pad. He wrote a one-page confession, neatly printing his letters on the lined, legal paper:

> In the morning I get up from sleep do
> this and that then my sister get a call
> from a male to come over he come
> over I'm getting anger. I do not like
> people from like that to come to my
> apt I'm getting more anger my sister comes
> to my room I had a gun in my hand
> and I went to talk to the man in my house
> and fired the gun. God help me.

He signed it Heriberto Seda. He underlined "God help me." The word "man" was underlined three times. Then he drew a cross at the bottom and put three number sevens at the top ends.

Powers tore off the confession and read it. He noticed Eddie had left out shooting at the cops. He asked him to do it again and include firing at police. Eddie agreed and began to write on a clean sheet.

The detective looked at the cross and interrupted Eddie's printing.

"What does this mean?" Powers asked, pointing at the numbered cross.

"That represents God's pure love," said Eddie.

"Okay," said Powers.

On the second confession, Eddie twice misspelled the word police as "polcie." Eddie, a product of the city school system, seemed to speak normally, but wrote like a little boy. At the bottom, he wrote the word "Repent" and printed his name, Heriberto Seda.

Powers began to wonder about Eddie. He thought the cross Eddie had drawn looked like one of the Zodiac symbols. He had zip guns in the Seven-Five, "Home of the Zodiac Killer," as the cops' T-shirts proclaimed, and he was a religious freak. But Powers was unsure. He looked at Eddie again, a skinny mope with bad penmanship, the kind of guy who used to get beaten up in school for his lunch money. Powers hadn't been on any of the Zodiac Killer task forces. Before he stuck his neck out, he wanted to ask an expert—like Joey Herbert.

Powers put Eddie into a holding cell and took the notes to the shooting scene. He found Tommy Maher first, and showed him the notes. Tommy told Powers the cross was very similar to one of the Zodiac symbols, which had three sixes. They found Joey, who was physically and emotionally exhausted from the hostage negotiation and about to leave for home. They went into Powers's car to look at the notes.

"Look at that," said Tommy, pointing to the cross.

Joey looked at the symbol and then read the confession from top to bottom. He looked at the letters, especially the "N" and "A" and the snakelike letter "S." It was like looking at his wife's handwriting, he knew it so well. When he saw the triple underlining, he got the Rush. Hollywood re-creates the feeling of the Rush with what is called a "zoom-tracking shot," in which the camera moves toward the actor and the lens zooms out. The result is a dizzying effect, in which the world seems to rush toward you and away from you at the same time. Joey was excited, but controlled his excitement. Suddenly, he wasn't tired anymore and he had a lot of work to do.

"To hell with the symbol," said Joey, whose face was alight and bright red, despite his effort at control.

"Look at the writing!" Joey said, staring at the page. "I may be a fucking asshole, but, as I'm sitting here, this is the Zodiac Killer! This is him! This is his writing!''

Joey could not believe that the first barricaded gunman he had talked out of a hostage situation, and the killer he had been searching for for two years, were the same person. It was incredible. He went into high gear and started alerting bosses and pulling out the stops. The first thing to do was call Louie at Brooklyn North Homicide. Louie Savarese had copies of all the Zodiac letters at home, which would be needed to compare the handwriting. Joey and Tommy rushed back to the precinct and called Louie.

"Louie, go home and get your letters," Joey said. "I think this is our guy." Louie raced home to Long Island, using his lights and siren to get through rush-hour traffic, picked up the Zodiac letters, and turned around and went back to Brooklyn.

The second thing they needed was good prints. They had to get "Major Case Prints" from Eddie, which were impressions, not just from the fingertips, but from the palms, the sides of the hands, and the sides of the fingers. He called Ronnie Alongis at headquarters in Manhattan, the fingerprint expert who had memorized Zodiac's skin patterns, and told him to stand by for prints that might belong to the Zodiac Killer. After Eddie was printed, Tommy grabbed the print cards, got in an unmarked car, and rushed them to One Police Plaza.

It was the first time Tommy had ever used lights and sirens to transport paperwork. By now, Tommy, Joey, and Louie's necks were sticking way out. A lot of bosses were involved and a lot of people were being held on overtime. If the prints eliminated Eddie, they would look dumb; they would be the cops who cried wolf.

Joey and Louie began questioning Eddie. When Louie stood over Eddie, he seemed to take up half the sky. His voice was loud, compared to Joey's polite tones. They began talking about the shoot-out. At first, Eddie was polite and cooperative. The investigators talked about Eddie's zip guns. They mentioned his previous arrest for carrying a zip gun.

Then they told Eddie they wanted to talk about Zodiac.

Eddie instantly stiffened in the chair. He avoided the detectives' eyes and looked at the floor. It was just the reaction they were looking for. Eddie said nothing, even when they told him they thought he was the Zodiac Killer. He didn't deny it. He was thinking. You could almost hear the gears spinning wildly in his head. He remained silent, but he didn't ask for a lawyer. He just listened as Louie talked about the murders, as if he were enjoying it. Eddie's downturned face occasionally jerked into an involuntary smirk, as if he were fighting the urge to smile, to put on a Happy Face.

The news that NYPD might have nabbed the elusive Zodiac Killer put Happy Faces on a lot of people.

New York Police Commissioner Howard Safir was hooked on police work as a kid—when his detective uncle bagged famous bank robber Willie "The Actor" Sutton and got his nephew an autograph "To Howard, from Willie the Actor."

When Safir heard that the twenty-eight-year-old Brooklyn man who shot at cops might be the Zodiac, his first reaction was that he was too young. Safir had been in California in the 1960's and immediately thought of the San Francisco Zodiac.

"No, *our* Zodiac," laughed Chief of Department Louis Anemone.

"Oh. Wouldn't that be nice? Keep me posted."

While Tommy waited anxiously at headquarters, Alongis examined the prints carefully and compared them to the latent impressions Zodiac left on the Central Park and *New York Post* letters. Then he did it again. He was sure they were the same prints—but he asked another print expert to confirm his opinion. The second print guy confirmed it. Alongis gave it to a third expert.

"If this is the guy, do you have to call anybody?" Alongis asked Tommy.

"Yes." A full inspector, the police equivalent of a general, was waiting by the phone back in Brooklyn.

"Well, it looks good, but don't call yet."

Tommy was jumping out of his skin. The third print guy told Alongis he also had no doubt the inky swirls from a palm and a finger came from the same hands. A smiling Alongis turned to Tommy.

"It's him. Make your call." Tommy was already dialing.

"Inspector, we got a hit on the prints!" Tommy said.

"You're shitting me?"

"No, sir, I'm not." Tommy hurried back to Brooklyn. They had prints, but the Zodiac Killer had yet to confess.

In Brooklyn, the inspector called Joey and Louie into his office and told them Eddie's prints matched those of the Zodiac Killer.

"We got him!" they both shouted together. For Joey, it validated a two-year obsession. For Louie, it was the end of a six-year hunt. But the hunt was not over—until the Zodiac Killer "gave it up." The inspector called headquarters and asked that the Zodiac Task Force files be unlocked and brought to the Seven-Five, as soon as possible. The Task Force files filled dozens of boxes, all marked with the Zodiac symbol. They were loaded into a truck and carted into the precinct on hand trucks.

When he got confirmation that Eddie Seda's prints matched the Zodiac Killer's, Commissioner Safir called Mayor Rudy Giuliani to give him the confidential news. He reached Hizzoner at the opera.

"It looks like this guy is Zodiac," Safir told Giuliani.

"You're kidding," said Giuliani, a former federal prosecutor. While the two were talking, one member of Giu-

liani's security detail told the mayor that he had just heard
the news on a local radio station.

"Why am I not surprised?" asked Safir.

The three investigators took a while to compose themselves. About 8:00 P.M., they walked back into the interview room, which contained only a bench and a table and
chairs. The walls were bare, except for a wide mirror on
one wall, which was a one-way mirror with an observation
room on the other side.

Louie strode over and shook Eddie's hand, as if he were
congratulating him. Eddie looked puzzled.

"We've got your fingerprints—you're the Zodiac,"
Louie explained.

"We have the fingerprints. We know you're the Zodiac," echoed Joey.

Eddie seemed startled and then his body seemed to sag.

"I don't know what you're talking about," Eddie said.

Good Guy Tommy sat close to Eddie and patted him on
the back, comfortingly. Joey urged Eddie to confess—to
say he was sorry and do the right thing—to cleanse his
soul.

But Eddie was not ready to give it up. For the next two-
and-a-half hours, Eddie and the detectives talked, argued,
and shouted back and forth.

"I don't have to be sorry for anything I did," Eddie
said with a sneer. "I only have to worry about it with
God."

Louie told Eddie he should be a man and confess. What
did he want people in the neighborhood to think of him?
His friend Tommy wanted him to tell the truth. Eddie
struck back with quotes from his Bible.

"Jesus and God are going to forgive me, not you," he
said defiantly.

"I'm at peace with God. I don't have to repent to you.
I only have to talk with God," he said, a smug expression
on his face.

The word Zodiac spread like wildfire throughout the department. Detectives suddenly found urgent reasons to go to the Sutter Avenue station house. It was as if a wake was being held at the precinct. Zodiac detectives were coming to see the guy from behind the one-way mirror and pay their respects to the detectives who got him. Detective Lieutenant George Rice could not believe Eddie, who looked to him like a little hubcap thief, was the Zodiac Killer.

"This is the guy who drove us crazy for six years?" he asked incredulously.

At 10:30, Joey told Powers to put up the crime scene photos of Joseph Diacone and Patricia Fonti so Eddie could see Zodiac's handiwork. He had run away so quickly after the shootings, he had never seen the obscene reality of death his bullets had caused. He had never seen his sleeping little dead. Powers taped the color, eight-by-ten-inch photos up on the wall.

Eddie saw the glazed eyes of Joseph Diacone glaring reproachfully at him. There were holes in his throat and blood everywhere.

"Who is going to speak for these people?" Louie boomed in a huge voice that could be heard outside the closed door.

"Somebody has to speak for her," Louie said, gesturing to Trish Fonti's corpse. Her back was painted with purple gashes. Her dead eyes also condemned Eddie. Her mouth was open wide and spewing maggots—like a sentence of damnation.

Eddie quickly looked away from the bodies on the wall, but his eyes couldn't help returning to them, again and again, as Louie's voice rumbled loudly.

"It isn't enough to say you are at peace with God. These people have to be at peace with God, too," Louie thundered. "They have to have their rest." He told Eddie that Son of Sam killer David Berkowitz apologized to the mother of one of his woman victims, and even serial killer Joel Rifkin said he was sorry.

"Are you more of a monster than them?" Louie asked. "Why should you go down in history as a bigger monster? That's not the kind of man you say you are."

Eddie lay down on the bench and Joey spoke to him in a voice as sincere as a parish priest.

"You're closer to the devil than you are to God, Eddie." He remained silent, but he was obviously affected. Joey and Eddie discussed human sacrifice and justifications for murder.

Eddie asked for his blue Bible from his room. Danny Powers went to get it for him and arrived back at the precinct around midnight. He gave the Good Book to Eddie, who, after a while, asked to be left alone for a few minutes, to read a Bible passage.

The detectives left him alone and Eddie flipped to a section in the rear of the Bible, near the apocalyptic Revelations of Saint John, a passage about human sacrifice.

They walked back into the room at 1:20 A.M. and sat down at the table with Eddie. He made them wait a few more minutes while he finished reading his Bible verse. When he was done, he looked up and made another demand.

"I don't want to talk to Louie. I don't want to talk to Joey," Eddie announced, indicating he would speak to Maher and Powers.

"I'll leave," said Joey, but he told Eddie that Louie had to stay "because he worked on the case the longest."

Reluctantly, Eddie agreed.

"Okay, let's start from the beginning," said Louie, who was poised to begin writing on a legal pad on the desk.

Eddie said nothing.

"Watch," whispered one of the detectives watching from behind the looking glass. "Now Tommy's gonna crack him like an egg."

Tommy gently clasped Eddie's shoulder, like the long-awaited touch of a father's hand. Eddie turned to Tommy, who smiled encouragingly at him. Eddie shot a glance up at the pictures of Trish Fonti, took a deep breath, and started talking.

"She was in front of the YMCA. I approached her. I wanted to get her into the park. I walked with her into the reservoir and offered her cigarettes. We walked into the place where I was going to shoot her. It was dark and foggy. I shot her and . . ."

"No, you didn't," interrupted Louie. "You didn't shoot her, you stabbed her."

"I'm telling you I shot her. I shot her and then I stabbed her. I fired and she fell. I went to reload and she . . ."

"Wait," said Louie, who was now also wearing a friendly smile. "Let's start from the beginning."

Eddie started at the beginning, with Mario Orozco, and began working his way through all of the Zodiac Killer shootings.

As he confessed to one shooting after another, Eddie also began to teasingly expose his long-secreted self, as if he were a human matryoshka doll, lifting shell after shell and offering peeks at the other effigies inside—and then slamming down the lid.

One of the Eddies inside was suddenly concerned about Chachi.

"How's my sister doing?" he asked, more than twelve hours after the shooting. He was told that she was going to be fine.

Eddie said that he had stalked Mario Orozco several times and knew where he lived. He revealed that he had left the zip gun, with a note wrapped around it, at the scene of the first shooting. If true, it meant the gun had been stolen before police arrived.

When he got the feeling, Eddie confided, he had to go out and hunt for new victims. He had a "lust" to kill, he said.

Louie asked Eddie if he was "aroused" during the

shootings, that is, did he have an erection while killing.
Eddie seemed offended by the question and his shell
clamped down again for a few minutes. After he had confessed to all of the shootings, they asked Eddie how he
knew the signs of his first four victims before he shot them.

He smirked and the lid came down again.

"I guessed. Some of them I got from watching television."

It was an obvious lie. No one, including the press and
the police, knew anything about Zodiac until after the third
victim, Joe Proce, had been shot. Zodiac wrote the signs
of the victims down on paper on or before the time of the
shootings. Mathematicians said guessing was out of the
question. Why was Eddie lying? Was he protecting someone? He also downplayed the occult and satanic aspects of
his letters and the entire concept of killing one person for
each astrological sign. He said he threw in "all that stuff"
to confuse police. The detectives didn't believe him and
wondered if he was afraid of what people, especially his
religious mother, might think of his alleged blood pact
with the devil.

They showed him a copy of Zodiac's first press clipping
from exactly six years before—the front page of a June
19, 1990, *New York Post*, "**RIDDLE OF THE ZODIAC
SHOOTER**," that had the first letter to the paper.

Eddie admitted he had written that and the other Zodiac
letters and had created the "looking glass" flag code. But,
when he was asked about using a mirror to create the symbols, Eddie seemed genuinely confused. How could the
Zodiac Killer not know how he created his own secret
code? Eddie said he got the code off a card he used to
carry in his pocket.

Louie wrote down Eddie's admissions, which took up
five legal-size pages. Eddie signed, or, rather, printed his
name on every page.

After the confession was signed, the big detective asked
the smaller confessed killer if he remembered the box

score on the 1994 letter to the *Post*, in which Zodiac claimed nine shootings to the NYPD's zero. Eddie said he remembered.

"You beat me for six years," Louie said with a big grin. "Now it's 'Zodiac zero, NYPD one'—with a real big smiley face!"

Eddie was not smiling.

Joey, Louie, and Tommy were ordered to report to the office of Police Commissioner Safir, known as "The PC," in a few hours, at 8:30 A.M.

"You did a spectacular job," Safir told them when they arrived. All three were promoted that afternoon, at a City Hall press conference attended by Mayor Giuliani. They were heroes. They were stars.

"First, the public should know that this kind of investigation is more than just a job to these officers," Safir said later. "They breathe, eat, and sleep this kind of investigation.

"They have to crawl inside the head of the individual they're pursuing and be smarter than he is."

Louie and Tommy and another detective took Eddie on a tour of the shooting scenes that day and Eddie pointed out where the crimes had taken place.

Other detectives from the Zodiac Killer Task Forces also interviewed the star suspect, and obtained more details of his life and activities. None of the alleged Zodiac confessions—over a thirty-hour questioning period without a lawyer representing the suspect—were written by Eddie. No audio or videotapes were made.

That evening, the Deputy Commissioner for Public Information, Marilyn Mode, went to the Seven-Five to see the suspect and arrange "the Walk," in which the detectives who broke the case got to walk the bad guy downstairs, out of the precinct, and past the cameras of the media horde gathered outside.

Mode was surprised at how little Eddie was when she

saw him through the one-way mirror sitting alone in a holding cell in the room where he had confessed to the most bizarre murder spree since the Son of Sam case. She and other officers watched him finish his takeout dinner of White Castle hamburgers and neatly fold the food wrappers into little squares. He wiped off the desk with a napkin and then leaned over and began doing something near the floor.

"Is he trying to secrete something in his shoe?" a suspicious captain asked.

Eddie was neatly picking crumbs off the floor. He was tidying up the cell.

"Oh, isn't he the perfect guest?" Mode laughed.

They let Eddie, dressed in dark pants and T-shirt, keep his blue Bible and cuffed his hands in front, so he could hold it and read it. Tommy took Eddie's left elbow and Louie took his right. Joey walked right behind them. It was warm and a drizzling rain was falling outside the station house, lit by bright lights from the TV cameras. Dozens of photographers, camera crews, and reporters were lined up behind barricades, waiting for the Walk, the killer's photo opportunity.

The press shouted questions at the silent suspect, most asking, "Why'd you do it?" They drowned out each other's words and elbowed for better positions. Cameras flashed and clicked. The meek, blinking young man named Heriberto—who liked to be called Eddie, Faust, and Zodiac—was escorted past the media, and off to Central Booking and jail, by three detectives sometimes called Big Louie, Porkchop, and Penguin.

Chapter 31

OLD WOUNDS, NEW WOUNDS

THE night Eddie confessed, Jim Weber started getting burning, agonizing pains from his Zodiac wounds. The scars marking the path of the bullet through his body—from his lower back to his right thigh—twitched with shooting pains, making it impossible to sleep. It was not the first time it had happened and Weber assumed it was the sudden rainy weather that had brought back the ache of the old wound. A spasm would subside and Jim would drop off to sleep, only to wake up in a cold sweat to another pang. Every time his wounds kicked up, it reminded him about the night he was shot by the laughing gunman, who was still out there.

Jim did not know that the wounds of the other surviving Zodiac victims were also throbbing that rainy night. He would not know until the next morning that Zodiac was out of circulation, if not out of his nightmares. *Post* reporters knocked again on the victims' doors.

When Diane Ballard saw a news report about the capture of the Zodiac Killer on television, she couldn't believe it. She never thought the day would come. Diane had to walk with a cane and take drugs for the rest of her life. She could not wait to testify against the man who gave her such pain and terror, who ruined her life.

She said that she was angry—angry that she could no

longer dance, angry that she couldn't even run with her young granddaughter. She began to cry.

"I'm scared to go out at night, I have my children go with me. Three years of my life have been taken away from me. I used to think 'live and let live.' Now I don't feel that way anymore."

Larry Parham never thought they would catch Zodiac and was afraid to believe it was actually over. If the Zodiac Killer was behind bars, he would sleep a lot better. He said he believed in punishment but forgave the gunman. He said he would like to "try to help him find God again." He also felt sorry for Eddie's mother and sister.

Mario Orozco seemed to be the only Zodiac survivor who was not completely traumatized or embittered.

"I'm happy every day." Mario smiled when asked if he was happy his alleged attacker had been arrested and had confessed. "I am not angry. I am not God. I don't have to forgive."

The shooting was predestined, he said.

"This is something that was written for me."

Dominic Proce, a cousin of Joe Proce, spoke up on behalf of his murdered relative.

"Poor Joseph went through hell and I hope this bastard they arrested has to go through hell as well. Joe was an old man, a veteran, and he deserved to live the rest of his life in dignity. Instead, he lingered in the hospital for three weeks before he died because some maniac shot him," said Proce.

"Thank God they finally caught him. May this finally be done with."

When she went to visit Chachi at the hospital, Gladys was surrounded by reporters and TV crews. She dismissed reports in the neighborhood that her children detested each other and that Chachi had recently asked a friend to kill her brother. Gladys told the press that her son "was a nice, quiet boy. Something in him must have snapped.'' She claimed she knew nothing of the huge arsenal in her son's room, or the bullet holes in his walls and ceilings. She could not believe Eddie was the Zodiac Killer, but, if he was, ''he has to pay the consequences.''

The day after she was shot, Chachi woke up in a bed at Brookdale Hospital after surgery. Her mother was holding one of her hands. The twenty-five balls of lead shot from her brother's homemade shotgun struck her in the buttocks, at the base of her spine. Some of the pellets bored into muscle, others ripped up her intestines, but they all missed her spinal column. Surgeons removed most of the metal from her body, but could not recover all the pellets, some of which would be eliminated naturally from her lower intestines.

Doctors opened up her abdomen and installed a colostomy bag, which she would have to wear for a few months. If she healed properly, she would be able to go home soon. Two more surgeries would be required to patch her up. When she started getting her strength back, she began to curse Eddie out.

''I hope that he rots in jail and never comes out. I hope he dies.''

It was boring in the hospital, especially because the TV set in Chachi's room was broken. On the fourth day, her elder sister Cathy came to visit her and told Chachi what Gladys had not—Eddie had been charged, not just with having an arsenal and shooting her, but with being the Zodiac Killer.

''Zodiac? What's that?'' Chachi asked. She had been eleven years old when the shootings started. When Zodiac returned in 1994, Chachi was only reading one thing in the paper every morning—her horoscope. Cathy explained about the Zodiac Killer, who killed three people, wounded five others, and thumbed his nose at the entire police department for six years with secret codes and weird satanic letters.

Chachi was dumbfounded—all this time she had thought Eddie had no ambition at all.

Chapter 32

GOOD BOOK, BAD BOOK

AFTER he was marched past the press in the rain, holding his blue Bible, Eddie was taken to Brooklyn Central Booking, the same place he had gone two years earlier for carrying a zip gun. The building was on Gold Street, near the Manhattan Bridge, just a few blocks from the Brooklyn Navy Yard, where the headquarters of the first Zodiac Task Force had been located.

But this time Eddie was a star.

"Hey, Zodiac! Did you eat those people? Are you another Jeffrey Dahmer?" taunted one arrestee in a nearby holding cell, as Eddie was booked. Other prisoners, like Johnnie Walker, jeered. A few threw food at Eddie, who—Good Book in hand—took the abuse serenely, like a virgin martyr in the arena.

"They were sinners. I was doing God's work," he told them.

Inside the holding pen, Eddie was approached by a twenty-year-old assault suspect.

"What can I do to stop me from sinning?" the youth asked.

"You should start by reading God's word," Eddie advised.

"What religion?"

"No religion, just God's word."

Police moved Eddie, for his own protection, after one prisoner growled, "Put that motherfucker in here with me and I'll show him what he can harm!"

In his own cell, he read his Bible and prayed fervently, never once picking up the pay phone on the wall to make a call. Eddie did not need to call anyone. He was already talking directly to God.

At 8:00 A.M. the next morning, Eddie was taken from his cell to go to court. He again suffered taunts and threats.

"We've got the Zodiac!" one accused felon shouted.

"Why'd you shoot your sister?" asked another. Some of the prisoners were released and spoke to *Post* reporters outside, who put it all in the paper.

Eddie did his best to ignore the street people. He was much more comfortable with law-enforcement officers like cops, or the white-shirted court officers at the holding pen in the basement of Brooklyn Criminal Court, where he was taken for arraignment.

"Why'd you do it?" asked one curious court officer.

"She was bringing boys into the house. They were drug dealers," said Eddie.

"What about the Zodiac shootings?" the officer asked.

"I needed attention. For once in my life, I felt important," said Eddie. "I was lonely, in pain. I have no friends." He talked about how his life went downhill after he dropped out of high school, how he became "impressed" with the military and began making guns. The officer asked Eddie why he stopped the Zodiac attacks.

"Because I found God. It's something I put behind me. I found God."

Eddie balked as he was about to enter the courtroom, because he saw cameras pointed his way. The place was packed with the press and Eddie was camera-shy. The officers told him he had to go inside, so he simply backed into the court of law, to keep his face turned away from the cameras. He politely greeted his court-appointed lawyer, Alexandra Tseitlin. Standing next to his pretty, petite lawyer, who was clad in a dress suit and wore her short chestnut hair in a crisp bob, Eddie almost looked big.

Clutching his blue Bible behind him, Eddie was arraigned on thirteen counts of first-degree attempted murder, for shooting at the cops, and one count of attempted murder in the second degree, for blasting Chachi in the butt. Tseitlin said her client was not guilty. She asked he be sent to King's County Hospital for a psychiatric exam. "This case," she told the court, "is being tried in the media."

Tseitlin, thirty-four, who took the high-profile case because she thought it might be interesting, represented Eddie on all charges filed in Kings County, also known as Brooklyn. She was excited by the case, and sometimes felt a little overwhelmed by it. Lawyer David Bart was appointed to represent Eddie on the three murder and one attempted-murder charges in Queens County.

One irony Eddie would find out about later was that Wilbur "Tush" Rios had been arrested and charged as Eddie's accomplice, because several cops believed they saw two different men shooting at them. The charges were later dropped.

Queens District Attorney Richard A. Brown got a call at home, early on June 19, that a suspect had been charged as the Zodiac Killer. All three Zodiac murders—Joe Proce, Trish Fonti, and Joseph Diacone, as well as the attempted murder of Jim Weber—were committed on Brown's turf, in Queens. He immediately ordered investigators and prosecutors from his office to the 75th Precinct. The Zodiac Killer case reminded Brown of the Son of Sam case, especially in the way both serial killers terrorized the city. In 1977, as a supervisory judge in Brooklyn, Brown had arraigned newly arrested Son of Sam serial killer suspect David Berkowitz.

At a press conference three days after Eddie was arrested, Brown talked about the vulnerability of the Zodiac victims. Later, he expressed his thoughts about Zodiac more directly:

"The son-of-a-bitch shot people who couldn't fight back."

Assistant District Attorney Jim Delaney handled the arraignment of Eddie Seda, but ADAs Kirke Bartley and Bob Masters were assigned to prosecute the accused Zodiac Killer, who was soon indicted.

Slim, soft-spoken Bartley, forty-seven, an experienced homicide prosecutor with a wry sense of humor, had recently been portrayed by an actor in a movie about convicted mob boss John Gotti. Bartley was amused that perhaps his worst moment in court had been immortalized on celluloid. He had been the prosecutor of the infamous "I forGOTTI" case, in which an alleged assault victim recanted his account on the stand. The man claimed he had a bad memory—when he found out the husky guy he had accused of beating him up was wiseguy John Gotti, who referred to him throughout the brief trial as "Pinocchio."

After one July Zodiac Killer court session, Bartley said that Zodiac "kept the whole city terrified" but was "not a particularly courageous serial killer." He felt the shootings were simply "thrill killings . . . sadism at its most basic."

Bob Masters, forty-one, joked one courthouse wag, is "so good looking, he can play himself in the movie." Masters had a head of salt-and-pepper hair and a matching mustache. His comments, too, had a bit of spice. "Eddie," Masters joked with a smile, "would hang upside down in his room like a bat" and emerge occasionally to shoot and kill victims. Masters was already digging into the stacks of Zodiac files that filled his office. He scoffed at the satanic and astrological trappings of the Zodiac Killer, but was himself secretly superstitious. If he had a case on trial in the old Jamaica courthouse, he did not take the elevator but used only the left side of the double spiral stairs to get to the courtroom, as he had on previous successful prosecutions. Masters said he and Bartley would prove Eddie was the Zodiac Killer "beyond a reasonable doubt."

The first-floor courtroom in Kew Gardens, Queens, where Eddie might face three murder charges, if he went to trial, had dark wood paneling all the way up to a high ceiling. The only stars in evidence inside the court of law were two gold stars of the republic—flanking the golden words "In God We Trust" on the wall above Justice Thomas Demakos's head. The Kew Gardens courthouse was in better repair than the old Jamaica courthouse a few miles away. One courtroom there was in such disrepair that some of the golden letters above the judge's bench had corroded and become invisible against the dark wood and seemed to read "In od We rust."

Watching the proceedings through gold-rimmed glasses, the silver-haired Demakos had a reputation as a no-nonsense jurist—short on formality but long on the law. But Demakos's informality did not extend to assigning Tseitlin as co-counsel. He refused. He told Bart he would allow Tseitlin to work with him "but I don't want to see both of you in the courtroom at the same time."

When Eddie saw his court-appointed lawyer, David Bart, walk into a Queens courthouse holding cell for the first time, he may have thought the chubby, bespectacled Bart was a gift from God. Eddie wished he had been born a Jew because he felt they were more committed to God. The quick-witted Bart, thirty-seven, was an orthodox Jew and wore a black yarmulke on his balding head. The skull-cap bobby-pinned to his wavy black hair was a token of faith, but Bart knew his Bible as well as he knew the law. At their first meeting, the easygoing Jewish defense lawyer and his quiet Christian client got along well and were over-heard discussing the nonlegal matter of the Song of Solomon.

The Song of Solomon is a collection of wedding songs sung by women and is the only book of the Bible that has romantic love as its only theme. In Chapter III, verse 2, the words, like those of many love songs, speak of longing and a search for love: "I will rise now and go about the city, in the streets and in the broad ways, I will seek whom my soul loveth: I sought him but I found him not. . . . The watchmen that went about the city found me, they smote me, they wounded me. The keepers of the wall took away my veil from me."

Eddie, an unmarried young man trying to win back the affections of his sister, might have found another one of the songs, in Chapter VIII, comforting: "Oh, that thou wert as my brother, that sucked the breasts of my mother. When I should find thee without, I would kiss thee, you should not be despised."

When he was arrested, Eddie emerged blinking and unshaven from the shadow of obscurity, dressed in his dark night clothes. After he had been pulled into the daylight world, Eddie adapted to his new surroundings. After a makeover that included a shave, shower, haircut, and wardrobe change to jeans and a polo shirt, the crazed serial killer suspect had been transformed into the boy next door. Queens courthouse lawyers joked that the first commandment for a defendant in a jury trial was "Thou Shalt Not Be Ugly." Bart, an avid poker player, told reporters that Eddie had been held incommunicado for thirty hours and grilled by dozens of detectives, many of whom came away with purported confessions that his client had signed—but not written. Also, said Bart, none of the alleged admissions had been recorded on audio or videotape. The only proof that Eddie said anything in those confessions, the lawyer said, was the word of overzealous detectives, who had been obsessed for years with catching the Zodiac Killer. He filed motions to have all the confessions thrown out. Bart had defended murderers before, but—like his colleague Tseitlin—Eddie was his first serial killer and his first high-profile press case. He knew that it was extremely unlikely that the DA's Office would allow his client to plea-bargain a deal, so bluffing was not in the cards. He wondered what other cards might be in the prosecution's hand—besides, that is, the four aces they already had: fingerprints, ballistics, eyewitness identification, and confessions. Was there a wild card in the deck? Later, he would discover there was—DNA evidence. Would DNA testing on the "letter lick" and "stamp lick" of the 1994 "Love" stamp, nail his client, or free him? DNA evidence certainly did not nail O. J. Simpson.

On July 26, Eddie acted as his own lawyer for a few minutes. David Bart was not in court because he had to rush to the hospital with his wife, Marla, after she went into labor with their fourth child. Justice Thomas Demakos asked Eddie if his lawyer had anything planned for a particular date. "Not that I know of," Eddie replied.

At his second court appearance in Brooklyn, Eddie sported charcoal-gray slacks, and a pinstriped dress shirt. "Chameleon is a good name for him," Joey Herbert said later. "He'll be in a tuxedo by the time of the trial." *Daily News* reporter Maureen Fan thought Eddie was handsome and resembled Pearl Jam rocker Eddie Vedder. At one point, Eddie, his handcuffed hands holding his Holy Bible behind him, looked up at the golden words above Justice Albert Tomei's head: "Let Justice Be Done, Though the Heavens Fall."

I came across the name of Emergency Medical Service paramedic Edward Tudor on a police report in a pile of court documents. Until it was made public as part of the pretrial discovery process, Tudor's name had never leaked to the press. The Manhattan EMS paramedic told police he saw a man near Larry Parham's bench in Central Park the night he was shot, June 21, 1990. When I contacted Tudor, he told me he was surprised that no one from the Manhattan DA's Office had gotten in touch with him in 1994 or in 1996, when the Zodiac arrest had been made. I was the first person who had contacted him. Tudor had heard about the arrest, but the pictures he saw on TV and in the papers were not good enough to tell if it was the same man. I showed him a full-face shot of Eddie taken at one of his later court appearances.

"Yeah, that's the same person I saw," said Tudor. "I haven't seen that face in six years. Wow. That's the guy I saw six years ago.

"It's chilling. It's spooky. At the same time, it's terrifying and fascinating," he said.

Only one surviving victim, Diane Ballard, got a look at Zodiac. There were at least three other witnesses—four, counting Tudor—but none had ever picked Eddie out of a lineup, because no lineups were ever held.

At a September court appearance in Brooklyn, Bart, the poker player, announced that he was considering playing the Joker. He said something may have snapped in his client and he was investigating a possible insanity defense of "extreme emotional disturbance." A defense psychologist, Alan Perry, Ph.D. had told Bart that Eddie, who celebrated his twenty-ninth birthday behind bars, was not schizophrenic, but suffered from a condition known as "Schizotypal Personality Disorder." The disorder described a peculiar person who might look and act strangely, act paranoid, and have odd, unshakable beliefs and magical thinking.

"He's not classically schizophrenic . . . he does not currently have hallucinations," said Bart. Legal observers felt it was a weak defense, at best. Perry told Bart that the schizotypal illness did not "rise to the level" where it would make Eddie not criminally responsible for his alleged crimes. Perry could not testify that Eddie was not legally responsible for his acts. A tearful Gladys Alvarado came to court for the first time that day, dressed in a flowing, becoming brown silk dress. But she became too emotional and left the courtroom to cry in the hallway. She missed seeing her son, who craned his neck looking for his mother among the spectators. Eddie's eyes stopped when he saw three familiar faces in the front row—Joey Herbert, Louie Savarese, and Tommy Maher. The beginnings of a smile played on Eddie's face, as he nodded toward the detectives. They were there to arrest him again. The new collar was an "in-custody" arrest for the Zodiac attempted murders in Brooklyn of Mario Orozco, Germán Montenedro, and Diane Ballard, for which he had just been indicted.

"It's not as exciting as the first time," joked a smiling Tommy Maher. It was unclear if the Manhattan DA would ever bother charging Eddie with shooting Larry Parham.

Beneath his summer suit, new artwork graced the crowded canvas of Louie's skin. The Zodiac Killer's drawing of himself in an executioner's hood, "Me in the Park," had been tattooed on the skin of Louie's right forearm, a memento of that eerie, misty morning in Central Park six years before. Inked onto the flesh of Louie's other forearm, like a living hunter's trophy, were two dates and one word:

March 8, 1990

Z⊕DIAC

June 19, 1996.

Of course, the "O" in Zodiac had been turned into a crosshairs Zodiac symbol, like a Celtic Cross graveyard headstone—marking the lifespan of the Zodiac Killer. As he displayed his new tattoos, Louie put on a happy face and smiled.

Gladys defended her son when I interviewed her and her daughter over the Labor Day weekend. She invited me into her neat apartment and spoke about Eddie, from his childhood up to his arrest. She told me she was "very hurt and shocked that he would ever do something like this." But then she claimed Eddie had been railroaded by the cops, who had browbeaten her exhausted son into a confession and denied him a lawyer.

"When they arrested him in the precinct, they kept telling him 'you're the one—you know you're the one,' without somebody being present to help him," said Gladys. "That's not fair."

She said her son once showed her one of his shipments of bullets, but maintained she knew nothing of the roomful of illegal weapons he bought them for. Gladys allowed me to look at Eddie's room and his personal effects and books, including the Moses magic book. I began flipping through the magic spells and incantations, trying to control the Rush, as I realized its significance.

"This is Eddie's book? He wrote in this?" I asked, as I saw the word "Faust" scribbled in the margins next to the magical spells.

"Yes," said Gladys, apparently unaware of its occult content.

She said Eddie read silently and aloud from his blue Bible, her white Bible, the Spanish Bible—and the Moses book. Chachi told me her brother prayed and chanted and talked to himself in his room for hours every day. I looked again at the Moses book, and the incantations circled in ink. There seemed to be oil stains on some of the pages, and a page on curing illness by ritual bloodletting had what appeared to be a bloodstain on the paper. I shouldn't have been surprised that a man charged with shooting people according to their astrological signs, and who used the names Zodiac and Faust, was performing black magic in his Brooklyn apartment—but I was.

During the interview, Gladys several times interrupted Chachi when she began to say negative things about Eddie or the family.

"Talk nice," she told her daughter several times, under her breath, in Spanish. Gladys was distraught over the scandal and didn't want to be known as the mother of the Zodiac Killer.

Because of the tension, I also later interviewed Chachi at a local diner. It was hard not to like the teen, who had an infectious ha-ha laugh and a pleasant disposition. She told me that a counselor had told her that she was suffering symptoms of Post-Traumatic Stress Disorder as a result of the shooting. Chachi had lost six pints of blood and twenty-five pounds from the shooting. Her colostomy bag had been removed and her abdomen was stitched up, but she faced one final surgery before she was done. She was very nervous, and the sudden noise of a beeper made her jump in her seat. A gun battle on a television show one night made her hysterical, she said. Chachi told me she was under pressure not to testify against her brother. She was also the only victim who had to take calls from the guy who tried to kill her. When she answered the phone in the kitchen in late August, she recognized a familiar voice she had not heard in months:

"Hello?"

"Hello." It was Eddie, calling home for the first time. She was terrified and furious at the same time. She immediately handed the phone to Gladys, who told her son to "be careful" in the cellblock with thirty-eight other prisoners. Unlike other accused celebrity killers, Eddie was not put into protective custody.

Like Freddy Krueger, Eddie was stalking his sister in her nightmares. The night after Eddie called, Chachi dreamt that they didn't press charges against Eddie and he came to the house and "pounded the shit out of my mother and then he set up a bomb in my bakery." Chachi stopped answering the phone after that nightmare, but she kept having more bad dreams. They were filled with blood and she and her friends died in them. The worst was the one where she went to sleep and woke up on the kitchen floor. Eddie was standing over her with a gun and this time he was going to kill her. She was frozen and her legs would not move. There was a loud boom, and the white floor was suddenly awash with red blood. When she was awake, Chachi loathed her brother.

"I want him to die," she said, remembering her night-mare. "He should get the chair. I would go to the funeral and laugh." She was disappointed to hear that, outside of her gangster books, there was no electric chair, and Eddie did not face the death penalty. Chachi then talked about ordering "a hit" on her brother in jail, apparently verbalizing a victim's fantasy of revenge. But, when asked whether she thought Eddie was the Zodiac Killer, Chachi was unsure.

"I don't know. In some ways, I don't think so. I doubt it, because he was never into that astrology. But if he shot me, he could shoot anybody in the street." Chachi said she was trying to resist pressure not to testify against her brother, to simply not show up if she was called to court.

"I'm going to press charges because he almost killed me. I will tell the whole truth and nothing but the truth."

Chachi said she wanted to get her high school equivalency diploma. Despite her street friends, she said her dream was to go to college, become a counselor for troubled teens like herself, and start a family.

"God made me to live for something and I want to find out what it is." She smiled.

Before he was transferred to a cell at Riker's Island, Gladys visited Eddie, who was under psychiatric observation, at Kings County Hospital. He spent his time there watching TV and reading his Bible in a room with bars on the window—just like he had at home for the previous twelve years, except there were no blue rose curtains on the windows to hide the bars.

"How are you?" a tearful Gladys asked her only son.

"I'm okay," said Eddie. "Mommy, how do you feel?"

"I'm okay," she said, through her tears. "How are you eating?"

"Okay." Eddie told his mom that he was no longer angry with his sister.

"I'm okay with Chachi," he said, magnanimously announcing that he forgave his sister and expected Chachi to forgive him. He never apologized for shooting her—or anything else. The word *Zodiac* was never mentioned. It hurt Gladys to see her son, who she also called by his childhood nickname, "Herri," behind bars. She cried and told him she loved him and missed him. Mother and son prayed together "for power" and Eddie read aloud from his blue Bible. Gladys prayed that her son would be found not guilty.

"Mommy, I'm okay. Don't forget about me," Eddie said.

She tearfully told her child she would never forget him.

"How is the house?" Eddie asked.

"Okay." Gladys told Eddie how the police search of his room had made a big mess and had broken the glass in one of his windows, which was now fixed. She told him about the boxes of stuff that cops took out of his room, leaving things behind, like his blowguns, in a huge pile of clothes and belongings.

He asked his mom if the searchers took his Moses magic book.

"No."

Eddie seemed suddenly hopeful and pleasantly surprised to hear that the cops had not removed his volume of sorcery—that contained spells like the one requiring salt and water and rose oil and promised the user would "depart without restraint" from his "judicial trial." He told his mother to bring the book of magic to him on her next visit, as soon as possible.

"I need it," Eddie told her.

Chapter 33

LOOSE ENDS

THE biggest remaining mystery about the Zodiac Killer is how he knew the signs of his first four victims.

The specter of an all-knowing serial killer stalking the shadowy streets generated real fear in New York. Thousands of police investigative hours and resources were spent trying to answer the question, without success. Detectives—active and retired—are still divided on the issue. Many are convinced Zodiac, or a witting or unwitting accomplice, had access to some kind of computer database that contained dates of birth. When suspect Eddie Seda claimed he guessed the signs or saw them on televison, detectives believed he was lying. Was the Zodiac Killer suspect trying to cling to the last shreds of mystery that remained of the Zodiac legend, or was he protecting someone? Perhaps neither. It is theoretically possible Zodiac guessed the signs, but very unlikely and no evidence of database access has been found. Unless you believe in a psychic Zodiac with supernatural powers, there is really only one answer left.

It may be an unpopular, non-glamorous theory, but I believe the Zodiac Killer may have learned the birth dates of his first four victims simply by asking one of them and looking in the wallets of the other three.

The first victim was Mario Orozco. It didn't matter what

the first sign was. Since he couldn't possibly be a repeat, it was possible to shoot first, and question his sign later. Mario said he felt like he was hit on the head, fell down, and played dead, while Zodiac pointed the gun at him. Zodiac stalked Mario, so it was possible he already knew his birthday, but I believe Mario was unconscious after he was shot and woke up after Zodiac had looked in his wallet and found his health insurance, or other identification, which gave his date of birth. When Mario regained consciousness, the gunman wasn't trying to take his billfold out of his pocket—he had just put it back. Zodiac was not a thief but few investigators believed Eddie Seda's claim that he left one of his cherished weapons at the scene of the first shooting.

The second victim was harder—now Zodiac had to look before he leaped. Germán Montenedro, on his way back from a party, was falling-down drunk, which may have made it possible for Zodiac to search Germán before he shot him—to make sure he had a different sign from the first victim. Montenedro's passport, with his birthdate on it, vanished from his coat. But Zodiac was so cowardly, I find it difficult to believe that he would get close to anyone he hadn't shot first. He may have shot his victim and then made the happy discovery that his gamble had paid off and he had not shot a duplicate sign. Only Zodiac knows for sure.

The third victim was Joe Proce, who was so confused he could not remember his own name or address. Zodiac probably just asked him his birthday, which he had celebrated just a few weeks before he was shot. Joe may have even given Eddie one of his ''cards,'' which contained Joe's name and address, perhaps even his date of birth and Social Security number. In fact, Joe may have been Eddie's first intended victim as long as six months before he was shot. The Zodiac message sent to the 75th Precinct in 1989 said ''the first sign is dead'' inside a Taurus pie slice. Perhaps Zodiac planned to shoot Joe first but shot

Mario instead after Joe failed to appear on the street alone.

The fourth victim, Larry Parham, who was known to take a drink, slept soundly on his bench in Central Park, after putting his wallet and identification under the bench, inside his sneaker—where a stealthy Zodiac could have found his birthdate before shooting him.

The idea of robbing his victims of their birthdays, but not their wallets or valuables, was actually quite clever and worked its intended magic—the police, the press, and the public were spellbound and mystified. He successfully performed his sleight-of-hand magic with the signs four times, but only killed three people. Zodiac was actually a better magician than he was a killer. Perhaps, as with fictional puzzles, no solution is as interesting as the mystery it answers.

Six Zodiac Killer victims and several eyewitnesses and police officers may be alive today only because the accused Zodiac Killer could not afford real guns on his tiny budget of loose change. The homemade one-shot zip guns were innaccurate and packed less punch than commercially manufactured multiple-shot weapons. If the Zodiac had gotten his eager hands on any of the heavy hardware advertised in Eddie Seda's gun magazines and catalogs, the body count would probably have been much higher and Zodiac would have gathered more sleeping dead into his fold.

After Eddie Seda's arrest, there was some talk in the police department and in the press that the detectives did not catch the Zodiac Killer—that Zodiac caught himself, by inking the triple-seven cross on his confession to the shoot-out. It is true that if Eddie had not allegedly drawn that symbol, events might have developed very differently. If the symbol had never been drawn, or Danny Powers had ignored it, Eddie would not have been questioned immediately about the Zodiac case. Perhaps, unlike in 1994, the zip guns would have been tested ballistically and found to be Zodiac guns, but many knowledgeable detectives doubt it. Even if police later discovered the Zodiac link, Eddie would have had a lawyer by then, and there would have been no alleged confessions to bring to court. It is sobering to think that had Eddie not drawn a cross and three sevens on a piece of paper, the Zodiac Killer suspect might have again become a ghost in the system. He might have been charged only in connection with the shoot-out, perhaps to emerge from prison and return to East New York after not too many years—convinced that his Zodiac magic was still working.

Fortunately, Powers didn't ignore it, and Joey Herbert, Louie Savarese, and Tommy Maher, along with other detectives, including Lieutenant Vinnie Mazziotti, Louis Pia, Richard Tirelli, and Robert Geis, achieved the kind of results that long ago earned New York City investigators the reputation as ''the Greatest Detectives in the World.''

But cops, no matter how good or dedicated, are not psychic. If they were, detectives from the first Zodiac Task Force would have known that a routine Zodiac suspect named Colin Ferguson would several years later become a mass murderer on a Long Island Rail Road train. Even if they had, without cause, grilled Ferguson and searched his Brooklyn apartment, they would have found nothing. Ferguson did not buy the black Ruger 9-millimeter pistol used in the attack until April of 1993. NYPD eliminated Ferguson as a Zodiac suspect after he was cleared by fingerprints, which cops got from the federal Immigration and Naturalization Service, which also then investigated Ferguson. In the paranoid, rambling note the hateful gunman had in his pocket on the night he killed six unarmed commuters and wounded nineteen others, Ferguson cited that INS investigation as one of the factors that spurred him to kill. I covered the LIRR Massacre and trial and Ferguson has written me several letters from prison, complaining of absurd, non-existent plots to poison him. After I inquired whether Ferguson knew he was a Zodiac Killer suspect, he wrote me an incoherent, paranoid 8-page letter from his upstate jail cell that made it clear that he believed all the police investigations, including the Zodiac investigation and my own, were all part of the racist plot against him by white people.

The Zodiac case inspired extreme theories, even after Eddie's arrest. Retired Swami Squad detectives Al Sheppard and Jim Tedaldi appeared with me on a CNBC television show and repeated their minority belief that the Zodiac Killer had help with the shootings and may have been part of a cult. Although it is possible Zodiac had help with his crimes, it seems unlikely, given his personality. I have seen no hard evidence that the shootings were the work of more than one person. I believe it is much more likely that suspect Eddie Seda was a cult of one. It is, of course, possible that one or more people around Zodiac knew some, if not all, of what he was doing—and did not report it to police, not an uncommon occurrence in East New York.

Before Eddie was arrested, one investigator had jokingly put forward a "spanking theory," in which the Zodiac Killer, who held a whole city hostage, stopped his shooting rampages both times because his mommy, or someone close to him, found out. After this hypothetical person discovered what Zodiac did on his midnight walks on Wednesday nights, the Zodiac got spanked and was not allowed out on Wednesday. But, the theory went, after a two-year grace period, the Zodiac began quietly shooting victims again, who were stalked or attacked on every night of the week—except Wednesday. Was the serial killer keeping his activities quiet because he was afraid of being discovered by the police, or someone else? In 1994, the attacks stopped as soon as they were made public in the *Post*. After his arrest, Eddie Seda said he repented in 1994. If true, it would mean the biggest deal in the Zodiac suspect's life may not have been the one he made with God or the devil—but with his theoretical confidante.

Or, did Zodiac enter the anonymous shadow of a church

confessional booth and confess his crimes to a priest, who would have urged him to stop killing? In the two years before his final arrest, during which he attended church, Eddie channeled his energies into becoming a police informant and antidrug crusader. But, whether he confessed his sins or not, no amount of praying or repentance could beat the devil out of him and he began stockpiling weapons and bombs for the coming, final apocalypse.

The spanking and confessional theories would make dramatic fiction, but Gladys Alvarado and all other family members denied any knowledge of Eddie's alleged activities. No evidence of criminal knowledge or behavior was found and they have never been charged with any crime. Eddie's parish priest, Father O'Malley, or any other Catholic priest, is bound by the seal of the confessional and would never divulge any sins that might have been confessed there. In that case, the only person who could ever tell would be Zodiac.

Also in the category of bizarre theories was the suggestion that there were more secret messages in the Zodiac letters. Zodiac buff Raymond Houston pointed out that the last four letters of the word Pleiades is "Seda" spelled backwards. I looked literally backwards and forwards through the letters and found no further code, but, of course, I am an amateur. However, in the 1990 "Me in the Park" letter, the first letters of the first two words in "Honi Soit qui mal y pense" are *H* and *S*—the initials of Heriberto Seda—and were the only letters in the phrase that had been capitalized. It may have been a simple coincidence or an unconscious slip of the pen. Only Zodiac knows for sure.

I consulted Manhattan handwriting expert Charles Hamilton, who compared the Zodiac messages to the confessions written by Eddie Seda in June 1996. Hamilton agreed with police experts and was convinced they were all written by the same person.

"They are definitely in the same handwriting," said Hamilton.

Eddie's lawyers have said they are exploring a psychiatric defense for the accused Zodiac Killer. A defense psychologist found Eddie was suffering from schizotypal personality disorder, which might be a weak defense, as opposed to a strong psychiatric defense such as schizophrenia or multiple personality disorder.

I also consulted Manhattan forensic psychiatrist Dr. Michael Welner, who noted that multiple personality disorder, the "Sybil" mental disease, is an extremely rare condition and was very unlikely. But Welner said if he were called upon to interview Eddie Seda, he would have to investigate the possibility of MPD, because of certain factors, including his different demeanor and appearance at different times. In his alleged confession, Eddie claimed he guessed at the signs. Is it possible that only "Zodiac"—and not Eddie—knew how the signs were obtained? Eddie Seda is right-handed, but victim Diane Ballard swears she saw Zodiac reach for his gun with his left hand. Is it possible that Eddie uses his right hand, but "Zodiac" is a southpaw? During the alleged admissions, Eddie expressed apparently genuine ignorance about how his own secret code was created. Is it possible that only "Zodiac" knows how he created the code? The inconsistencies are intriguing but far from conclusive and the defense has made no claim of multiple personality disorder.

Eddie Seda's psyche certainly might be at issue in a trial, but his saliva might prove to be stronger evidence against him. Authorities believe the DNA from Eddie Seda's spit will prove he is the Zodiac Killer. His body fluids—especially saliva—would have to be drawn and compared to the PCR, or polymerase chain reaction, test results obtained in 1990 by the FBI and by the NYPD in 1994. Even if they matched, the odds would only be one in seven Hispanics. However, other more specific testing could be performed by the prosecution on the Zodiac envelope or stamp "licks." Further testing might isolate a sample with much higher odds, perhaps even astronomical numbers, that might impress a jury. It would certainly be ironic if Zodiac's arrogance—in choosing and licking a "Love" stamp for his letter to the *Post* about his murders—sealed his fate.

At a trial, Diane Ballard and Edward Tudor, among others, might be called to the witness stand, to point a finger at Eddie as the Zodiac Killer. A documents expert would be expected to testify that Eddie wrote the Zodiac letters, several of which were left at the scenes of shootings. Detective Ronnie Alongis would be called to testify that Eddie Seda's fingerprint matched at least fifteen points of Zodiac's fingerprint, more than the ten required. A ballistics expert would be expected to testify that Zodiac's clever use of guns without spiral grooves inside the barrels was, in fact, not clever at all. The bullets may have been actually easier to match than rounds from a regular weapon. The Zodiac bullets looked smooth to the naked eye because they did not have the lands and grooves of a slug fired from a normal gun. Lands and grooves were useful, but the individual characteristics of a gun barrel were reflected in the microscopic scratches underlying them. The prosecution expert would be expected to say that, unlike store-bought weapons, the markings from Eddie's homemade firearms were unique and matched Zodiac slugs fired into Jim Weber, Larry Parham, and Joe Proce. At a trial, Joey Herbert, Louie Savarese, and Tommy Maher, along with other detectives, would be called to the stand to swear that Eddie confessed he was the Zodiac Killer, even though he never said the actual words 'I am the Zodiac Killer.' In addition, a carload of physical evidence—from a table full of zip guns and ammunition, to grisly crime scene photographs, to a Brooklyn telephone book riddled with bullet holes—would be brought into court and shown to a jury. Before they rendered a verdict, that same jury would have to examine the bizarre, satanic Zodiac letters, and then look at Eddie Seda and decide whether the polite, handsome young man at the defense table went around shooting people in the back because he thought he had sold his soul to the devil.

Eddie Seda pleaded not guilty to all charges and is innocent until proven guilty in a court of law. He stands clothed in a cloak of innocence, as the lawyers say. But the defense team of Alexandra Tseitlin and David Bart, who were keeping their cards close to their vest, looked overworked and worried at some of their court appearances. Their smiling client, however, seemed serenely unconcerned, as if he knew something they didn't.

When last seen, the Moses magic book was at 2730 Pitkin Avenue. For me, it was the missing link between the Bible, astrology, "Faust," and the satanism of the case. Perhaps it might be helpful to the defense, who could use it as evidence of Eddie's possible insanity. I do not know whether Gladys brought the book to her son in jail, as he requested, or whether he might actually be allowed to practice the Black Arts with it in a city correctional facility.

If, sometime in the future, after a "judicial trial," he emerges from the courtroom and is able to "depart without restraint" from the courthouse and out into the relatively fresh air on Queens Boulevard, it might prove either that Eddie Seda was not guilty—or that the magic works.

EPILOGUE

THE surviving victims of the Zodiac Killer are trying to get on with their lives, but many can't.

Mario Orozco continues to work and still socializes with his friends in the neighborhood, just yards from where he was shot. After the June 18 shoot-out, Mario found out that the friendly girl behind the counter at the local bakery was the sister of Eddie Seda. The first victim left a message at the bakery for Chachi Reyes while she was hospitalized. He wanted to speak to her. Chachi was understandably hesitant to contact one of her brother's alleged victims, but apparently Mario simply wanted to express get-well wishes to her. After all, now that she had been shot by the accused Zodiac Killer, the teenager and the grandfather had something in common. They were the oldest and the youngest survivors.

Germán Montenedro no longer talks to anyone, outside of his family, about the night he was shot and what it did to his life.

Larry Parham is still troubled by that night in Central Park but is comforted by his Christian faith, which tells him to forgive Eddie Seda.

Victim Jim Weber's Zodiac wounds, like the other victims', still attack him with pain when the sky darkens with rain. He has started to sleep a little better at night, but still trusts no one and cannot work.

Victim Diane Ballard also cannot work but is looking forward to walking into court with her cane and pointing out the man she will swear is the Zodiac Killer. She hopes that confronting the man with the evil eyes will give her some kind of closure to three painful years and exorcise those evil eyes from her dreams.

Eddie Seda is now inmate 8325275M on Riker's Island. In his first jailhouse interview in September 1996 Eddie spoke to TV producer Roger Keyes and *Post* columnist Steve Dunleavy wrote about it. The accused Zodiac Killer asked for forgiveness from the survivors and the victims' families.

"If they can forgive me from their hearts, they in turn will be forgiven by God for the sins they have committed," Eddie said.

"My messages come from the Bible," he said. "You know, in many ways I wish I had been born as a Jew. I am a Christian, but Jews, you know, they seem to have a much greater commitment to God, like they are more serious about it than others."

Eddie is still a star behind bars and prisoners ask for his autograph. He seems confident that the weapons confiscated at his apartment will not prove he was the Zodiac Killer.

There would be no ballistics evidence without a gun barrel, which could vanish after a shooting "if you kept changing the pipe," he said.

Eddie, who faces a maximum sentence of $83\frac{1}{3}$ years to life behind bars, if convicted on the three murder and one attempted murder charges in Queens alone, is resigned that he may be spending the rest of his life in a cell, but he does not seem concerned that the earliest he might be free would be when he is one hundred and thirteen years old.

"Yes, I will be in prison, a place like this for the rest of my life, probably. No, jail doesn't bother me. It's a prison in here, but it's a prison out there. I have no trouble in here.

"Anyway, wherever you are, Earth is only a waiting room for heaven."

In 1996, some irreverent members of a women's journalists' group unofficially voted the handsome Eddie Seda their "most fuck-able perp of the year" award.

Father Sean O'Malley prays for Eddie Seda and the parish was planning to reach out and offer him help in jail. When asked how one so religious might be capable of such terrible acts, the man of God sighed.

"Only God knows."

Gladys Alvarado and her daughter Chachi Reyes still live in the apartment on Pitkin Avenue. Conflict over Eddie still divides them. Gladys visits her son in prison and Eddie calls home, trying to speak to Chachi. "I want my sister to forgive," said Eddie. "She doesn't talk to me, but I'm working on it."

The defense team of David Bart and Alexandra Tseitlin are busy preparing Eddie Seda's case for trial. Prosecutor Bob Masters was expected to try the case after his colleague Kirke Bartley was nominated for a judgeship. In November 1996, Brooklyn Supreme Court Justice Albert Tomei threw out two shooting cases against Eddie Seda—Mario Orozco and Germán Montenedro—because the statute of limitations had passed.

Television weatherman Al Roker was surprised to learn in 1996 that two cranks had called the Zodiac Task Force in 1990 and said he was the Zodiac Killer. "Maybe they didn't like the forecast," Roker chuckled.

Author Kieran Crowley is still a *New York Post* reporter, covering Long Island and the Queens courts for the paper and working on a new book. He will cover the upcoming triple murder trial of Eddie Seda.

Former army code-breaker Al Nemser continues to practice law on Long Island.

Retired Swami Squad detectives Al Sheppard and Jim

Tedaldi are private investigators, working as technical advisors on a new TV cop show for Warner Brothers and NBC TV, called *Prince Street*—based on their years in NYPD's Intelligence Division.

Detective Bill Clark retired off "the Job" and became a consultant to the hit TV series *NYPD Blue*, which won high praise for its gritty, realistic portrayals of working New York City detectives. When he got a call from a former colleague about the Zodiac arrest, Clark uttered a detective's prayer: "Please, God—don't let it be anybody we looked at." His prayer was answered. Clark is now an Emmy Award–winning television and movie producer, living in Santa Monica, California.

The 1990 Task Force never heard of Eddie Seda. One detective in the 1994 Task Force who did hear of Eddie Seda, Louie Savarese, had the satisfaction of locking him up two years later.

Detective Ray Liebold is retired and lives in rural Pennsylvania. Deputy Chief John Menkin is retired and living in Florida.

Detective Sergeant Mike Ciravolo also retired, as a Lieutenant, and is now president of Beau Dietl & Associates, a private investigation and security firm in Manhattan.

Chief of Detectives Joseph Borrelli retired in 1995 and always regretted that the Zodiac Killer was not bagged on his watch.

"All my buddies on the Job would always say, 'You were the guy who nailed the Son of Sam but you couldn't get the Zodiac Killer,'" Borrelli said from his Lynbrook, Long Island, home, after Eddie Seda's arrest.

The thirteen police officers involved in the gun battle with Zodiac Killer suspect Eddie Seda, many of whom contained the gunman with return fire and protected civilian lives, were not promoted or given medals or transfers by the NYPD for their bravery. As per routine, they have themselves applied for commendations through department channels, and are awaiting a reply.

On October 7, 1996, Joey Herbert, Louie Savarese, Tommy Maher, and Danny Powers went to the auditorium on the second floor of One Police Plaza with their proud families. Police Commissioner Howard Safir presented each detective with the police Centurion Award, for their work in capturing the Zodiac Killer. Joey, Louie, and Tommy received promotions for their work.

Tommy Maher still works as a detective in the Seven-Five Precinct and still hates the nickname Penguin. His favorite hat is an old baseball cap bearing the Zodiac symbol and the words "The 75th Precinct—Home of the Zodiac Killer."

Louie Savarese still works as a detective in Brooklyn North Homicide but now sleeps very well at night.

Joey Herbert was given the command of his own detective squad in Brooklyn's 75th Precinct. He is still a dedicated detective, but his only obsession now is the quality of hockey played by the New York Rangers. When a recent caller asked what was new, Joey shrugged and replied with a characteristic smile and quiet humor:

"Nothing, just doing God's Work."

Amen.

CHRONOLOGY

- NOVEMBER 17, 1989: First Zodiac letter, "This is the Zodiac," warning of twelve murders to come, is mailed to police five months before the shootings begin.

- MARCH 8, 1990: First victim Mario Orozco, 49, a Scorpio, is shot in the back with a 9mm zip gun on Atlantic Avenue at the intersection of Sheridan Avenue in East New York, Brooklyn at 1:45 A.M. Seda later claimed he left the zip gun with a note wrapped around it at the crime scene, but it was never found.

- MARCH 29, 1990: Second victim Germán Montenedro, 34, a Gemini, is shot in the side with a 9mm zip gun at the intersection of Jamaica and Nichols Avenues at 2:57 A.M.

- MAY 31, 1990: Third victim Joseph Proce, 78, a Taurus, is shot with a .38-caliber zip gun in front of his home on 87th Road in Woodhaven, Queens at 2:04 A.M. A Zodiac message was left on his front porch.

- JUNE 4, 1990: Zodiac mails his first letter to the *New York Post* from Brooklyn. "This is the Zodiac. The twelve sign will die when the belts in the heaven are seen."

- JUNE 21, 1990: Fourth victim Larry Parham, 30, a Cancer, is shot in the back with a .38-caliber zip gun while sleeping on a bench in Central Park at 3:52 A.M.

- JUNE 21, 1990: Zodiac mails a second letter to the *New York Post*, with the "Me in the Park" drawing of Zodiac in a hood, after shooting Parham.

- JUNE 24, 1990: Third shooting victim Joseph Proce dies at Jamaica Hospital.

- AUGUST 10, 1992: Fifth victim Patricia Fonti, 39, a Leo, the first woman victim, dies after being shot with a .22-caliber zip gun and stabbed over 100 times on the shore of the reservoir in Highland Park at 1:50 A.M.

- JUNE 4, 1993: Sixth victim James Weber, 40, a Libra, is shot in the buttocks with a .22-caliber zip gun at the corner of Vermont and Cypress Avenues outside Highland Park at 12:04 A.M.

- JULY 20, 1993: Seventh victim Joseph Diacone, 40, a Virgo, is shot in the neck and killed with a .38-caliber zip gun at Vermont and Cypress Avenues outside Highland Park at 11:35 P.M.

- OCTOBER 2, 1993: Eighth victim Diane Ballard, 40, a Taurus, is shot in the neck with a .22-caliber zip gun while sitting on a park bench at 1:13 A.M.

- MARCH 10, 1994: Seda is arrested at 10:45 P.M. in front of his Pitkin Avenue home by Officer Brian Fleming, who confiscates a .22-caliber zip gun. The weapon is incorrectly labeled inoperable by the police lab and is never tested.

- MARCH 18, 1994: Seda is released from jail. Because he had no previous criminal record, the charges are dropped. His arrest record is sealed and his fingerprints are destroyed.

- JUNE 11, 1994: Zodiac claims he shot a ninth victim, a white man, in the head with a .22-caliber zip gun in Highland Park at 11:09 P.M. Zodiac may have missed or only slightly wounded the man. Detectives have been unable to confirm the shooting.

- AUGUST 1, 1994: Using a "Love" stamp, Zodiac mails a third letter to the *New York Post*, containing a new list of victims and nine mysterious totem-pole symbols—one for each victim claimed.

- AUGUST 8, 1994: The *Post* cracks and publishes Zodiac's secret code. His message: "Be ready for more," but Zodiac vanishes.

- MARCH 1995–MARCH 1996: Seda, "Doing God's Work," helps Officer Kathleen Vigiano by ratting out drug dealers in his building and in the neighborhood. Twice he quizzes her about the Zodiac case, "Did they ever get anybody for that?"

- JUNE 18, 1996: Eddie Seda shoots his sister Gladys Reyes, 17, in the back and barricades himself inside his mother's East New York, Brooklyn apartment, shooting at cops. Seda is convinced to surrender by Detective Sergeant Joseph Herbert, who served on the second Zodiac Task Force. Herbert, along with Detectives Louie Savarese and Thomas Maher, take Seda's alleged confession that he is the Zodiac Killer.